Lean Six Sig
Simplified

How to Implement the Six Sigma Methodology to Improve Quality and Speed

PUBLISHED BY: Greg Caldwell

Table Of Contents

Introduction

This book contains a detailed explanation of the Lean Six Sigma principle.

This book is for executives, leaders, and managers who are looking to keep their businesses profitable by maximizing employee productivity while conversing company resources. The Six Sigma Methodology provides businesses with techniques and strategies that will increase productivity and reduce overall waste.

Readers will be provided with solutions that can easily be understood and implemented. This book will also provide what companies stand to gain when they apply principles of Six Sigma. There will also be a section on the common mistakes made and how avoid them.

Thanks for purchasing this book, I hope you enjoy it!

Chapter 1 Introduction to Lean Six Sigma

What matters the most when in a business?

Any person who has ever been into a business venture or project has encountered that question from time to time. And, if you think about it, there are a lot of things that do matter in a business. This includes the organizational structure of the business, its policies, and its people.

Those are all noteworthy issues, there's no doubt about that. But there is one other aspect that any business person should never overlook: the process.

Why the process? The reason is simple. The process is the manifestation of a company's vision and goals. If the policies are the standard, then the process is the mean by which those standards are made manifest.

And every business who has ever produced something will always be judged by two things: input and output. To be more specific about it, a production is gauged whether it is good or not by how it maximizes the available resources while producing goods and services that are of noteworthy quality. In essence, a good producer knows how to maximize their efforts and optimizing the value that they offer.

And this is where your product methodology comes in. But that does leave us with a question: What kind of methodology are you using for your business, if any? What guides your production from step 1 to 139? What quality should the end product possess once the production cycle is complete? How much items should your company even create for that project?

Here's a scenario: imagine that your company creates and assembles engine components for various clients. Let's say that you got an order for 32 engine parts to be delivered within 5 months.

If your company built 65 engine parts, did you truly meet the project goals or were you wasting a lot of effort by producing more than what was asked? Did every item go through sufficient quality assurance checks before being shipped out? You have to remember that you were only asked for 32 components so did you actually meet the project goals without overextending your resources?

Or what if you produced the exact amount ordered but incurred several delays in the production process that spans weeks or months. No matter how good those components are, they would still not have meet the project specifications and you, of course, lost some valuable clients.

This constant clash between producing good quality, delivering on time, and minimizing unnecessary byproducts is something that could stress out any business owner. And you have to remember that resources are finite no matter how many they are. Eventually, and if you are not careful, you'd bleed out precious materials through overproducing and over-processing.

Undoubtedly, you have been trying or looking for different methodologies to guide your operations. But, if you are the one that is looking to optimize every move your business makes in the production process and optimize the results, then perhaps the Lean Six Sigma methodology might be the best solution for you.

What is the Six Sigma methodology? Without giving away too much right now (since you're going to read about it later on anyway), the Lean Six Sigma methodology was designed to help business optimize how their production processes for a single project or multiple ones by streamlining the process.

This way, at least on paper, your company should be able to provide more value to the clients while eliminating unnecessary waste, regardless of what form that takes.

At the same time, the process also focuses on building up on where your team is the most effective at. Continuous improvement of the current business layout should allow for organic growth for the company as it takes on bigger, more elaborate projects in the future.

But how should you apply it for your project? Like all other methodologies, Lean Six Sigma is only applicable in certain conditions, but the good news is that the methodology has a rather wide range when it comes to compatibility with project types and production process.

All that is necessary, then, is for you to find out how you can implement the method to your current business layout. This includes identifying your goals, understanding your current processes, and finding out potential areas for improvement.

In addition to this, you should understand that Six Sigma is not exactly the most fool-proof system out there. If one is not careful, it is easy to encounter pitfalls and create mistakes during the production process. Fortunately, such problems can be easily addressed so as long as you are quick enough to identify and act on them.

Of course, you might be asking yourself: is the process complicated to apply? The answer is no. To make things easier to understand, I have set everything up so that you learn the process step by step. Some situations based on real-world scenarios would also be provided so that you can understand that the process is highly applicable in real life.

And if that is still too complicated for you, don't worry. The truth is that the Lean Six Sigma methodology is not as demanding a process compared to other methodologies. It works with what you have and helps you improve on your overall performance based on where you are the strongest.

And, of course, the methodology is highly open towards change. By acknowledging the more unpredictable elements of the process, you can optimize your system to address change and come up with something that meets the new standards without making too much waste.

The point is that the process is highly sustainable and allows for multiple opportunities for improvement down the line. The more you adhere to the Lean Six Sigma methodology, the better you are in addressing its core issues while also applying its principles.

And if you have no further questions, now is the time to prepare yourself as we step into the world of the Lean Six Sigma Methodology.

Chapter 2 Some Preliminary Considerations

As was established, Lean Six Sigma is a process that is designed to streamline your operations on a continuous basis. The premise is that the constant cycle of improvement in how you produce value to your clients should make your business more capable of delivering on what it promises to its clients on time.

However, what you might not have known is that Lean Six Sigma is actually a hybrid concept. To put things simply, Lean Six Sigma is the combination of two concepts named, well, Lean and Six Sigma. To prevent some confusion later on, it is best that we tackle the basics of the concepts first.

What is Lean?

The most basic definition of Lean is that it is a process that aims to reduce waste and wasteful activities in a production cycle. In essence, it focuses on eliminating the steps in a process that are wasteful, either replacing them with ones that do or just simplifying the entire process.

Lean as a process is highly effective when it comes to:

- Reducing the time for each process cycle.

- Improving the delivery time for products and services.
- Reducing the chances that defects would occur in the production process.
- Reducing inventory levels while maximizing space.
- Optimizing available resources through strategic improvements in the production process.

Lean is also cyclical in nature. This means that it primarily promotes a continuous method of improvement in the systems and facilities in order to remove waste.

What is Value under Lean?

Value is a rather vague term when you think really think about it. However, Lean keeps things simple and just defines value is anything that is related to how a customer perceives a product or service that you are offering to them. And this just does not limit itself to customer perception but would also factor in their willingness to pay for such.

To put it simply, Value is the thing that people are looking for in your products and services to the extent that they would go out of their way to pay top dollar for it. And, in the production process, value dictates what steps must be included in it. Of course, a process is simply any activity wherein base materials are turned into components and components turned into actual products or services.

As a matter of fact, Lean defines several categories that processes can fall under. They are as follows:

A. **Non-Value Added Activity** – These are simply the activities that do not add value to the product or service. In short, they are wasteful steps that must be removed from the overall production process.

On the customer's perspectives, NVAs are activities that they think are not paying for when they purchase what you offer. In fact, if they know that such wasteful steps are included in the process and at a considerable amount, their perception of the product decreases considerably.

B. **Value-Added Activity** – These activities add value to the process and are deemed essential. They are steps that either improve productivity and quality or simplify the process, so things get done at a far more efficient rate.

C. **Value-Enabling Activity** – These activities are not something that the customer expects to pay for when they are purchasing your products/services.

However, they are integral to delivering value in the production process.

Believe it or not, every production process out there is comprised of 80-85% Non-Value Adding Activities. In short, there are quite a lot of unnecessary steps in a process aimed to turn raw materials into something tangible and functional.

The aim of Lean, then, is to identify these steps in the process, eliminate them, and simplify the entire cycle.

Waste and Removing it

The Lean traces its origins to the Toyota company through its Toyota Production System. The TPS model is something that was designed for production environments where a high volume of raw materials are to be processed to create an equally high volume of products as ordered.

However, Lean now can be applied to various environments because of its strong focus on waste, specifically process waste. Using the Japanese word "Muda" which translates to "garbage" or "useless" in English, the Lean method has identified several wastes that could be generated in any process. They are as follows:

- **Defects** – Inherent flaws in a product/service that occur in the middle of their creation.
- **Overproduction** – The facility simply creates more than what was necessary or demanded by the client.
- **Waiting** – This is the time spent by materials, resources, people, information, and equipment being idle as they are still not needed. This could also include the time necessary to set up important phases of the development process or the time spent processing valuable data.
- **Non-Utilized Talent** – Primarily a Human Resource based waste, this occurs when the company does not properly leverage the skills of their workforce. This includes placing people on positions where they are either underqualified or overqualified.
- **Transportation** – These are wastes that occurred when transferring equipment, materials, and personnel from Points A to B and onward. An important aspect here is that the movement itself does not add value to the final product or service.
- **Inventory** – The storing and stockage of unnecessary materials. This includes works in progress (WIPs) and other unfinished components.

- **Motion** – These are unnecessary movements of equipment and personal that take up time, energy, and other resources but do not necessarily add value to the product. Worse, they can result in work fatigue which decreases the productivity of the workforce.
- **Extra Processing** – This is where all the NVAs of a production process should be included once identified. Aside from that, any activity or task scheduled for a period such as performing work beyond what was specified by the customer should be included here as well.

The Principles of Lean

In order to be applicable for various projects and industries, Lean has adopted a rather simplistic process. In fact, these steps would form the pillars of the Lean movement and they are the following.

1. **Define Value** – You'd think that this process involves you identifying the value that your product has to its customers, but it doesn't. The thing about value is that nobody else (including you) can define it but the end user himself.

Identify your customers. Who are they? What problems do they face? What solutions to those problems can your product/service offer?

Upon identifying what your customers expect from the product, you can then start classifying them into the Non-value added, Value Added, and Value Enabling groups.

2. **Mapping the Value Stream** – So how does a raw material turn into a working product? What steps does it take? This will show that as you map out all the necessary steps that must be taken to materials and components into the end product.

This is also where you can identify all those NVAs and eliminate them. This should help your company reduce potential delays in the process while also improving the overall value of the product you offer.

3. **Create the Flow** – Once the stream of production is identified, you must then identify how that product is going to be delivered to your customers. The point here is that flow must be continuous so that the company can identify when and how to deliver on its promises on time.

The flow must also be designed to maximize the efficiency of the process. This means that unnecessary motions must be reduced, and wasteful activities avoided at all costs.

4. **Establishing Pull** – meet system beat time, which is simply the rate of which a product is created and optimized to meet the demands of the customer.

This is where the tool called Just in Time (JIT) comes in as it helps in establishing the pull through ensuring a work flow smooth enough that disruptions are completely done away with. This also helps in addressing inventory management and space-related issues.

5. **Seeking Continuous Improvement** – Lastly, your team must establish a sense of consistency in all of your processes. Constant effort for efficiency in terms of delivery time and product quality should be ensured, while also preventing the team from going back to older, inefficient standards.

By continuously improving, your business can identify more areas that generate waste and reduce the amount of defects and quality-related problems with your end product.

Six Sigma Defined

Alternatively, Six Sigma is a methodology that focuses on solving problems and is heavily reliant on cold, hard production data. Where Lean focuses on eliminating waste, Six Sigma primarily focuses on reducing defects and imperfections in the end product.

The Goal

Six Sigma has a rather bold goal. To be more specific, every product that you create under the Six Sigma system should have a 99.99996% quality rate. This means that the process you use should have only 3.4 duds out of a million good products or, better yet, less.

Six Sigma is best done with the use of the DMAIC system. DMAIC is an acronym that stands for:

- **Define** – Problems and objectives in the production process must be identified and set.

As such, it is important to create the project charter in this phase. This is basically a blueprint that the six sigma system would follow. It would also include:

- Business case

- Goal statement
- Problem statement
- Project scope
- Timelines
- Resources
- Estimated benefits

In essence, the charter is an outline of how the six sigma system is going to be implemented in the project.

- **Measure** – What is the current state of the production layout? What can be done to make it better? What are the metrics for success in this particular production process?

The variables in the process are going to be measured, hence, the process data will be analyzed and collected.

Once done, the baseline should be established, and metrics set. When compared against the final performance metrics, the overall process capability for the project can be identified.

- **Analyze** – The existing process and production system must be scrutinized. The goal here is to identify the factors that influence success, failure, and the generation of defects in the production process.

In this process, it is necessary to perform a root cause analysis. This can be done by using complex analytics tools to identify what caused a defect in the product. References like Pareto charts, histograms, fishbone diagrams, and other graphical data will come in handy at this point of the process.

- **Improve** – Come up with strategies that can enhance the systems and processes and then implement the improvements. The steps must include identifying, testing, and implementing solutions to a problem, and this can be done through simulation studies, design experimenting, and prototyping, among other analytical technics.

- **Control** – Once changes are made, the challenge then is to make them sustainable. Come up with policies and processes that make sure that your team does not slack off and go back to the older standards. This is to ensure that improvements are continuously seen in their output.

In other words, a control system must be put in place to monitor the performance of everyone in the project post-improvement. Also, a response plan must be done to address failure if ever it occurs.

One other important task here is Process Standardization which will guide all of your employees that handle the production process from this point on forward. This can be done through the setting up of policies as well as a manual that would instruct people how to conduct each process in the development cycle.

Finally, benefits will be reviewed here and estimated if they were met. All in all, this part of the process is focused on making sure that whatever gains were made during the improvement phase are not lost over time.

Similarities and Differences

Obviously, you must not conflate Lean with Six Sigma since they are entirely different frameworks. However, that does not mean that they don't share similarities or, better yet, complement one another. After all, why would you think anyone would bother combining them into one tool if they are not compatible with each other?

Just keep in mind that the differences are there to ensure that there is no shortage of available analytical tools and strategies that could improve your processes even further. And as for the similarities, they are there to drive home the point that Lean and Six Sigma can be done simultaneously or, for the purposes of this book, under a unified framework.

A. Similarities

- Both are reliant on the definition of value which is based on customer experience and perception. In short, the customer is the King.
- Both use a flow mapping approach to easily understand how the process could be improved. Even if the analysis is focused on the product or service, the end goal is still to make improvements on the process wherein such product or service will be made and delivered.
- Both rely on data when determining current performance as well as the impact of future performance. This is why the data collected in Lean Six Sigma can still be used in to support either of its parent frameworks.
- Both are applied using improvement projects that will be implemented typically in a cross-functional team. The duration of a singular

project and the composition of the team under both framework is determined by the scope and scale of the project.

- Both were primarily designed for manufacturing process but have adapted into other processes.
- Ultimately, either framework is highly effective in reducing waste and variation, whatever form either takes.

B. Differences

- Lean is focused on waste while Six Sigma focuses on Variation or any deviation from the target standards or performance.
- Lean uses visual techniques for analysis and problem solving and is supported by extensive data analysis. Six Sigma is more statistical in nature which is supported by data visualization. In essence, Lean is visual while Six Sigma is numerical.
- A lean solution is always supported by a value stream map. This would then lead to changes in work flows as well as work instructions through various steps in the production cycle.

Alternatively, the Six Sigma solution is supported with changes in the setup procedures and the control plan for monitoring the process to prevent deviations from the standard. This will also impact work instructions and would frequently lead to changes in the measurement approach and other similar systems.

These differences and similarities just emphasize that they have always been compatible to one another. As such, it is easy to merge them into one methodology that allows you to minimize your waste as well as deviations from the standards in your development process.

What is Lean Six Sigma?

And now we come to the most important part of this chapter.

Lean Six Sigma is a system that is driven be facts and data that is focused on preventing or minimizing defects in the end product while also eliminating whatever is considered as wasteful in the production process. It is something that is purely driven in minimizing variations in the cycle, eliminate waste, and improving the overall perception of the public towards the product or service.

And to do this, Lean Six Sigma combines the philosophies and principles found in its parent frameworks. To put it simply, it is designed to make the production process more efficient which, in turn, should translate to a better product. And not only do improvements occur on a one-time basis, they must be done continuously and whenever necessary.

Why Has it Become Important Today?

You might be asking "why is Lean Six Sigma becoming popular today"? The answer lies in the fact that the world has become much more dynamic today than it was in the past.

Shifts in fields like technology, economics, politics, and even culture means that consumer behavior can change at the drop of a hat. And not only do people like different things in a short period of time, the tools and technologies that you deem are superior today can become inferior in a moment's notice.

To better explain this, here's an example. Supposed that you are creating a videogame that runs on a graphics engine that allows for 1080 frames per second gameplay. What if, in the middle of your development, that graphics engine was rendered obsolete by an even more powerful engine that runs on 2040 frames per second?

Or what if an ambitious project was just dropped on your team and you must deliver on the vague promised features within 18 months or so? And, in the middle of the process, the people higher up decided to add new features or systems on top of what you are already working at.

Under normal circumstances, you and your team would be tempted to drop everything that you have worked so far and start from scratch. This means you'd be incurring delays, not meeting project specifications, and losing a valuable client in the process. And, as far as videogames are concerned, there are too many examples of such situations including Anthem, Mass Effect: Andromeda, and the infamous ET game from the 1980s.

The Lean and Six Sigma systems cannot meet such dynamic demands on their own, even if they are rather effective frameworks. As such, the most sensible option was to integrate the two frameworks into a singular but more comprehensive tool.

As was previously stated, the ultimate objective of Lean Six Sigma is to eliminate waste, reduce variation, and ensure a continuous improvement of systems and the end product. How the process can be effective is dependent on the project and your business's current layout. However, there is no doubt that the framework will ultimately help you in streamlining your processes.

As proof of that, Lean Six Sigma is used in various industries and sectors today, not just in car manufacturing where they originated from. Whether oriented towards products or in providing services, Lean Six Sigma has found a home in many businesses and corporations today.

The Takeaway

To summarize things, Lean Six Sigma is a methodology that works best if you are particular about eliminating waste and variation in the processes for your business. In essence, it is an integrated method that takes the best of what Lean and Six Sigma have and using them to great effect.

If done right, lean Six Sigma is particularly effective in improving process efficiency, optimizing resources, and satisfying customer expectations. And, of course, it is so adaptable that it has seen use in various industries today.

What that simply means is that Lean Six Sigma has worked well for others which means it can work for you. The only challenge, then, is to make sure that you implement it properly for your project.

Chapter 3 The Lean Six Sigma Principles

As of now, you might be asking yourself "What makes Lean Six Sigma effective?"

Just like its parent methodologies, Lean Six Sigma is guided by several principles that would determine whether or not is implementation is successful in your business. If you want your business to get optimized with its processes, it is best that you get acquainted with the following principles.

I. Addressing a Real-World Problem

By design, Lean Six Sigma is a methodology that focuses on the process from top to down and from bottom to top. The top-down aspect is often associated with the identification of a tangible issue in the process and then addressing it with the best possible strategy.

Lean Six Sigma is always focused on not only problems but problems that have continuously impeded a company's production processes as well as the overall reception of the end product. More often than not, the team will have to address such major problems through repairing and overhauling the production process while also addressing customer complaints.

In essence, Lean Six Sigma is not there to make people busy for busyness sake or to apply the proverbial band aid on a deep wound. It's there to apply something that would address an issue once and for all.

Did you remember the Quality Circle programs which were all the rage in companies during the 1980s? Basically, the premise was that the team has the full autonomy in choosing what projects they focused on.

This is all well and good for empowering a team and giving them ownership over their work. However, more often than not, teams had the tendency to choose problems that are surface-level or are mere symptoms of something greater. In essence, they are not addressing the root cause of the issue.

For instance, you run a restaurant that has been floundering for years. On the analysis phase, you found out that the problem points to the product i.e. the services and food that you offer. Perhaps the food is sub-par, your wait staff are not responsive, or the overall state of your kitchen is an utter mess.

So, how do you go about solving the problem? Do you renovate the place and add new equipment? Do you retrain your team to provide better food and services? Do you hire new chefs or wait staff? Or do you just lower the prices and offer discounts?

Only you can answer that dilemma but let's just say that the solutions that directly address the core problem most certainly does not involve gimmicky promotions.

The point is that Lean Six Sigma is there to offer your business a chance at real improvement. An actual overhaul, if you may, instead of a mere makeover.

But here is the problem, though. It is often hard to get an organization to recognize just how important it is for the methodology to succeed in order for the entire business to succeed. It is here where your ability to diplomatically tell your staff why it is important to change without dictating them what to do next will come in.

II. Team-Based Analysis

Cross-functional collaboration is a key aspect of the Lean Six Sigma methodology. The reason for this is quite simple: business processes, no matter what they are comprised of, are always cross-functional by nature. This means that every aspect of the process must correlate to one another and this is all the more important when it comes to analyzing problems in the process.

To put it simply, it is not enough to enhance a step. If you improve one aspect of the process at the expense of another, you are not exactly eliminating waste nor are you removing the probability of defects in the end product. You just made the problems move to another, and sometimes weaker, aspect of your production process.

And this is where the Lean Six Sigma methodology will encounter a lot of problems during implementation. Leaders, for instance, tend to find and address a problem on their own without informing the rest of the cross-functional team.

This might be permissible if the project is small in scope and the group composition is no more than 10 people. But in projects that are larger in scope or in cases where the leader has no previous experience with the process being analyzed, doing things on your own can be time-consuming or, worse, disastrous.

This is why Lean Six Sigma insists that you get the cross-functional team involved with the analysis. By having multiple people doing the analyzing with you (or for you), you can draw from a wider pool of knowledge and look things from different perspectives. In paper, this means that you can come up with a more comprehensive solution to a problem.

III. Process Focus

As of now, you should realize that the Lean Six Sigma method is best used for analyzing process. In fact, even if a problem being investigated points towards the product being the main source, Lean Six Sigma will address the problem by changing the process that designs, builds, and delivers the product.

The reason for this is that Lean Six Sigma is meant to analyze and improve on actions which, in turn, is part of the overall process. Actions do not happen for no reason and rarely do they leave no impact to succeeding steps.

As such, you are best not ignoring every action that occurs and why they are made. And if you think that's complicated, don't worry. This is where the Value Stream Map is going to come in and you'd learn more of that later on.

With a Value Stream Map, everybody understands what's happening every phase of the process and how they correlate to one another. With this, you and your team gets an understanding as to the underlying problems that are otherwise hidden if you look everything from an isolated point of view.

For instance, if you recognize that there is a defect in the product, the Lean Six Sigma allows you to approach the problem through correlating the product with the steps that made it in the first place. Perhaps the fault was created on step 3 which was carried over in the succeeding phases. Once identified, you can now single out the problem and address it. It's like surgery; just with less blood and more charts.

IV. Data

Lean Six Sigma is not a predictive framework. It does not rely on guesses (even calculated ones) but instead insists that you use data that can be verified and supported. Things like the current condition of your business's setup, the state of the production facilities and equipment you have, and the quality of the product and service that you offer are going to be scrutinized in the Measure phase.

In essence, Lean Six Sigma focuses on what is actually happening and not what you THINK is happening or might happen. It only through identifying the current state of things that you can hope to understand what must be fixed to make things better.

And, of course, data is not just for identifying problems. Once a solution has been mapped, data will then be gathered to determine if that solution is properly addressing the issue or not. And if it does solve the problem, data will be gathered again to find out how to make the solution sustainable or build on what has been achieved.

Why is data that integral to Lean Six Sigma, you ask? Here's the answer: no matter how you think you are transparent or open to change, the reality of your business's current state is often a tough pill to swallow. It may not be you per se or your team, but businesses often have a tough time accepting the fact that there is something wrong with their place.

Think of it this way: if you tell somebody that what they are doing is wrong, more often than not they'd resist the idea. But, if you come in heavy and present them with indisputable data through charts, graphs, and visual ideas, the more logical portion of their brain can put two and two together and come to the conclusion, for themselves, that what they are doing is wrong.

Simply put, you cannot hope to inspire change in your data by mere words alone. You have to back your claims with numerical and scientific data to appeal to the more reasonable part of your organization. If done right, this could lead to them making the necessary paradigm shift and implement sustainable changes.

V. Solutions that Address the Root Cause

Some methodologies start with the assumption that every problem has a unique or special cause. And if that cause can be identified, eliminated, or controlled, the problem will go away.

There are other methodologies that start with the assumption that the problem is a naturally occurring element within the process i.e. the process itself is flawed. And if the process were to be changed, the problem will go away.

To be truthful, both approaches are effective, if not admirable. But Lean Six Sigma understands that the best way to fix a problem is to put in place a system where problems can be easily spotted first. This, in turn, can control the occurrence of that problem or give way for the overhaul of the entire process.

And in order to make sure that the solution does not make things worse, Lean Six Sigma uses tools that can help you identify whether a problem is unique to your current layout or is a generally occurring one across businesses and production processes similar to what you have.

By making this distinction, your team can go about finding and isolating the root cause of the problem. Once identified, the team can create a solution strategy that will properly address the issue.

For a common cause, your team has the option to redesign the entire process, eliminating unnecessary steps and activities. If the problem is more special in nature, then a more laser-focused solution is needed.

VI. Making Solutions Sustainable

Lean Six Sigma is a methodology that is not content with identifying a problem and then solving it. The final phase of the process is something called Control, and this is where the challenge of keeping changes sustainable comes in.

You must expect resistance to come in all forms when implementing changes. Why is this so? Because, for many people and organizations, change is hard and uncomfortable. Security is best expressed in stability. The longer something remains as the status quo, the more comfortable people are in working along those systems and standards.

And this is can be a tough obstacle to deal with when implementing changes under the Lean Six Sigma method. New information has to be learned, old habits broken, and new methods have to be mastered. And while the rest of the organization is doing that, your team must also monitor how the implementations are carried out while setting up support systems, so everything does not revert back to the old standard.

In essence, you do not declare a victory under the Lean Six Sigma method just because you identified the root issue and came up with a winning solution for it. If the solution was successful once, the challenge then is to make it successful for a thousand times more. Consistency and sustainability are the two major indicators that whatever solution you came up with works and that the people behind the project are capable enough of applying it.

The Main Takeaway

Although these principles form the core of the methodology, you are not exactly required to follow them to the letter. They are only there to guide you to understand what needs to be improved on your business and how you go about bringing about those improvements.

As a matter of fact, you can have your own principles based on those mentioned above to guide how your staff goes about implementing the methodology. However, you must understand the intentions behind Lean Six Sigma and these principles do explain why things must be done in this way or that.

By understanding the "spirit" behind these principles, you and your team can come to an agreement as to how Lean Six Sigma can be applied under your current layout. After all, you are not expected to succeed in doing anything without first understanding why you should focus on certain aspects or perform certain tasks.

Chapter 4 Benefits and Other Matters

Lean Six Sigma is promoted as a continuous improvement methodology. However, you might have a question that can boil down to this phrase "Improve on what?" Does the method improve product sales and increased customer engagement? Does it lower complaints due to defects or poor deliveries?

What about the human resource side of things? Will it improve employee morale? Can it make the workplace more conducive to individual development?

The answer to all of these is one big "YES". But, to make things simpler, let's look at the more general benefits that a well implemented Lean Six Sigma strategy can bring to your business.

I. Organizational Benefits

The methodology was primarily meant for organizational application unlike other methodologies, especially Agile. As such, you can expect for the methodology to bring some tangible advantages for your organization which would include the following.

A. A Simplified Process

A direct result of eliminating waste and variation is that the overall process used by your business gets optimized. And by optimized, Lean Six Sigma means simplified. The cross-functional value stream maps will identify areas where waste is created the most, remove them, and create rework and workarounds for more persistent issues.

Once the waste is removed and the workarounds are no longer needed, what you would end up with is a process that is simpler and easier to manage. What happens, then, if the process no longer has unnecessary steps?

For starters, things get done faster now and end products can be delivered on time more consistently. This also leads to products of better quality which results in higher customer satisfaction ratings and, of course, increased sales.

Also, the faster process will lower overhead costs which will increase your profit margin.

B. Fewer Errors

The Lean Six Sigma process always starts with you defining what quality is acceptable for the entire project. This is of course based on what customers perceive to be valuable to them. This external focus on quality puts great emphasis on continuous improvements which makes the method effective in addressing actual root causes in a problem.

Also, the reliance on hard, irrefutable data over predictions and instinct will drive home the point that this method is all about solving actual problems, not just surface-level ones. The end result then is that the improvements implemented are more effective in addressing an issue while bringing the quality to a level more acceptable to customers. In essence, Lean Six Sigma is used not just to address problems. It is there to address the problems in your business that matter the most.

C. Better Performance Predictability and Control

It goes without saying that simpler processes are easier to control and manage than complex ones. The reason for this is that simplicity does away with variation which makes things even more predictable. To be more specific about it, the method helps you get better control on the process's cycle times, output quality, and overhead costs.

Think about it this way: If a process involves 3 steps, the chances of your staff mucking things up are fewer. Compare this to a process with 7 steps and 5 sub-processes where the margin of error is wider.

And when you make your processes more predictable and controllable, you give your business a tremendous advantage especially if you operate in an industry who has a nagging tendency to change standards from time to time. The Tech sector, for example, is quite notorious for consistently pushing the boundaries which means companies have little time to adjust to new tech standards before a new one is introduced.

Aside from changing technology, customers nowadays can be fickle which creates an even more unstable environment to do business on. With a predictable and controllable process, your business can adapt quickly without losing any momentum of sorts.

D. Active Control

Lean Six Sigma shortens cycle times and puts in control plans and support systems that are based on real-world data. And if you have short cycle times and data-based control systems, you and your staff are at a position to make better decisions that impact the way the entire process performs and at a faster time too. This should help in improving performance while also making boosting the morale of your team.

Aside from that, operators can now understand how their work can impact the overall process while also getting instant feedback. With this, operators won't feel like they are not in control with the process as they now can directly manage the process and also improve on it.

And with shorter cycles, the organization is better equipped to respond to changes in the marketplace. This means that you can make the necessary updates to your process to meet new standards without overspending or making things complicated again.

II. Personal Benefits

Lean Six Sigma is something that must be applied on an organization level and has benefits that cover the same scope. But what about the individuals that make the implementations happen? What does the method offer to them on a personal level? Here are some of its personal benefits.

A. Personal Effectiveness

Lean Six Sigma has always been about solving problems which means that operating under it makes you even more competent in any position and industry. The methodology guides you through a clear-cut process that involves inquiry, identification, and solution creation.

In fact, you don't have to be a manager of some big-time company to even apply Lean Six Sigma. The tools that it offers to you can be applied on everyday situations, not just scenarios found in board room meetings and production facilities.

And even if you don't use all the tools given to you, the Lean Six Sigma process will make you more inclined to assert greater control in finding problems and fixing them. In essence, Lean Six Sigma might be a business method, but its application is practically unlimited.

B. Leadership Opportunities

The methodology was designed for project implementations and projects naturally require leaders. In Lean Six Sigma, not only is a manager required to exercise all their leadership skills, but they are given the chance to be exposed to other functions and departments within the organization. Of course, the exposure comes in the context of finding and addressing a real issue in the process.

Constant interaction with teams will improve your communication skills while directly addressing changes in the marketplace trains in you making strategic decisions at a moment's notice.

And, if you do succeed under Lean Six Sigma, you open yourself up for advancements in the organizational chart. After all, what would make the higher ups be more receptive of your presence than the fact that you led a project which helps them save on expenses, improved their product, and reduced unnecessary by products in the production process?

C. Higher Pay and Upper Movement

Here's one benefit that the Lean Six Sigma method can offer to all of its practitioners: Credentials. The method has a "ladderized" system of certification. The more "belts" you get, the more qualified you become (for any higher-paying positions).

The reason is quite simple on a management perspective. Lean Six Sigma is easy to understand but there is a certain challenge to its application. Those that do manage to implement it effectively for projects gives higher ups an impression that they are ready for bigger responsibilities.

Of course, that promotion comes with its perks which always includes a higher salary. The rate may vary from one industry or country to another but it's easy to say that LSS certified people tend to land more rewarding jobs. As such, if you are the one that wants to quickly move through the ranks of your organization, then mastering Lean Six Sigma might help you do just that.

But what if you are already on the top of the organization chart? Since there is technically no upper movement possible, Lean Six Sigma is highly effective in making sure that your tenure in the organization is secured. It does this not through some underhanded, political maneuvering but through an honest, concerted effort to overhaul things below you so that they bring about the best of everyone in the organization.

In essence, by bringing about necessary changes and overseeing their implementation, you put yourself in a position where people can attribute whatever benefits they are reaping from the method to you. It's one way of making sure that you stay where you are in the organization for as long as humanly possible.

Where is Lean Six Sigma being used?

Right now, you might be wondering as to what industries and functions have Lean Six Sigma been used. The short answer is "Everywhere". Here's the more comprehensive answer, if you are wondering:

As was stated, Lean originated from Japan's automotive industry and Six Sigma from a high-tech system manufacturer. What this means is that Lean Six Sigma found its home in manufacturing industries. However, it was found out that the method can also be applied for other projects that do not necessarily revolve around process engineering and quality control. Here's a list of departments where the methodology has also found a place in:

- Logistics
- Information Technology
- Legal Services
- Maintenance
- Marketing
- Research and Development
- Sales
- Customer Service
- Human Resources
- Finance
- Engineering
- Product Testing

And Lean Six Sigma has also extended its reach into several well-known industries across the world including:

- Agriculture

- Aviation
- Banking and Finance
- Electronics
- Government
- Educational Services
- Healthcare
- Medical Products and Services
- Mining
- Energy
- Pharmaceuticals
- Retail
- Transportation
- Telecommunications

What Does this All Mean?

So, what does these benefits and wide range of applicability in Lean Six Sigma mean to you? For starters, it should give you the idea that the methodology is highly applicable regardless of what project you are undertaking in whatever industry that you are working on. As a matter of fact, you don't need to be that business-savvy in order to have an appreciation of what Lean Six Sigma has to offer.

Second, the methodology is potentially effective in addressing issues in your organization while also making its output better. All that is needed, then, is for you to understand how the process should be implemented into whatever system you currently have for your organization.

Chapter 5 Ranks, Tools, and Techniques

So far, you have been told why Lean Six Sigma is good and what guides it. However, you might be asking yourself now "When will I get to know how it's going to be done?"

Fortunately for you, that time is now. And to fully understand how the methodology is applied, you'd have to know the different ranks, tools, and techniques that are made available to you and your team.

Lean Six Sigma Ranks

The methodology takes a lot of cues from its parent Six Sigma framework as far as rank naming conventions are concerned. To put it simply, Six Sigma took its ranking names from Japanese martial arts.

In short, think of your team as a Karate Dojo; just minus the bamboo flooring and the need to punch somebody in the face. And since this is based on Karate, each rank has its own set of required training and certification.

Each organization used to set their own standards when it comes to applying Lean Six Sigma in the past. However, most groups today refer to the standards set by organizations like the American Society for Quality and the International Association of Six Sigma Certification.

Also, you don't have to use these names for your group per se if you find them a bit corny. Just get familiarized with what responsibilities each rank has to take in order to pull off Lean Six Sigma right.

A. The White Belt

This is where everyone who wishes to master the Lean Six Sigma methodology starts with. And just like in martial arts, Lean Six Sigma white belts are novices. The concept has just been recently introduced to them which means that they have yet to master any skill, tool, technique, or even principle.

As far as your Lean Six Sigma project team is concerned, White Belts should not take any active role as their focus is to complete the basic program. However, there is no harm in letting them try out simpler tasks such as gathering data to assist the higher ranks.

B. The Yellow Belt

Forming the base line of the Lean Six Sigma hierarchy, the yellow belts serve as the primary implementation agents of the method for various projects. As they are the starting rank, anyone who wants to become a yellow belt must simply learn the basics of the methodology and its various tools and techniques.

- The yellow belters are expected to take part in team meetings and would serve the role of a subject matter expert for their assigned function. Of course, that function is to be exercised in tandem with their full-time job.
- Depending on the size and scope of a project, there can be more than 3 yellow belts that form part of the team. Some of these yellow belts would have to divide their time performing tasks for multiple project teams.
- Training for yellow belts would mostly focus on the structure of the methodology and the use of various cross-functional tools and techniques.
- For analysis, the yellow belt is mostly relegated to assisting the green and black belt through collecting pertinent information. However, they may be able to help in interpreting the results provided that they already have the skills for it.

- Yellow belts are primarily required to lead the implementation of a solution within their own function or discipline.

C. The Green Belt

Like the yellow belts, green belts can also be numerous within an organization and usually serve the role of a project leader. The green belt is expected to work on Lean Six Sigma projects that fall within their own areas of expertise.

And since this is one rank higher, a green belt is expected to have mastered the basic Lean Six Sigma methodology and structure. They are also capable of applying the analytical tools and strategies for their respective projects.

- The green belt would lead various small projects that focus on one function or area of the entire business process. This is also performed in conjunction with their full-time job.
- Most green belts would also lead projects that is associated with improving one aspect of the business process. But there are also cases where green belts can take part in large cross-functional projects often lead by a black belt.

- As the project leader, the green belt will do the analytical portion of the Lean Six Sigma process, often leading it or observing the work of yellow belts.
- As the leader, the green belt is also expected to make sure that Lean Six Sigma is implemented properly and the tools and techniques it uses are employed appropriately.
- At Phase Gate Reviews, the green belt will do the presentation of data and the subsequent discussions. Their advanced training under the Lean Six Sigma methodology also means that that they are the most capable of interpreting the information they are presenting for the rest of the team or organization.
- The green belt is not exactly the subject matter expert for all aspects of the Lean Six Sigma implementation process. However, they can be an expert for some part of the process, product, or service.

As such, they can bring their expertise in the discussion the same way that a Yellow belt does. But that does not mean that everyone must expect for them to know everything about the process. And if they do encounter a problem in implementing a solution, they can turn to the black belt for advice and instruction.

D. The Black Belt

Organizations can have multiple black belts, although not as numerous as green and yellow belts. The black belt serves as the subject matter expert for a specific function or location within the organization. They are tasked with leading large cross-functional projects while serving as mentors for green and yellow belts within a particular group or department.

As a black belt, a person is not only required to master the basics of the Lean Six Sigma methodology, but they must also know how to appropriately apply the same. A black belt's day would include the following tasks:

- Conducting a team meeting for one of the projects that they are leading.
- Meeting with green and yellow belts to review what progresses they have made and provide instruction for the next steps.
- Performing an analysis on the value stream map for one of the projects that they are leading.
- Provide training for prospective green and yellow belts regarding the Lean Six Sigma methodology and tools.
- Meet with the organization's stakeholders, leaders, and even clients to discuss the status of the projects

that they are leading. They must also identify various issues and problems which must be avoided in future projects.

Clearly, the black belt is expected to lead various projects simultaneously while acting as a mentor for the ranks below them. The projects that they lead are also large in scope and cross-functional by design.

However, the most challenging part of their "duties" would have to be dealing with many different stakeholders. And once they do complete several projects, a black belt must be reassigned to a new function or department so as not to stagnate in their position.

E. The Master Black Belt

The last level of the Lean Six Sigma method, the Master Black Belt serves as the one managing the entire initiative of implementing the method in the organization. Unlike the previous ranks (and like Connor Macleod from Highlander), there can only be one Master Black Belt for every Lean Six Sigma organization.

Master Black Belts are full-time position and it comes with a number of responsibilities which include:

- On the perspective of training and certification, there is actually nothing that distinguishes a master black belt from your regular Lean Six Sigma black belt. However, their responsibilities are larger in scope and reach.
- The master black belt will not be managing a particular project. Rather, they are going to make sure that the Lean Six Sigma initiative is maintained for as long as possible.
- Master Black belts normally work closely with senior management to determine how many black, yellow, and green belts are needed and which functional departments and locations would get them first.
- They are required to maintain a status portfolio of projects. Here, they will detail what projects have been completed, which ones are currently being implemented, and what has been proposed in the most recent meetings.

In relation to this, they are able to assess the impact of the overall Lean Six Sigma program on the organization and they can determine which improvement efforts must be prioritized depending on what strategy the organization agrees to.

- The master black belt also work with the Human Resources department to maintain training records of all yellow, green, and black belts currently operating in the organization.
- If an organization is rather small or the Lean Six Sigma initiative is limitedly applied, the role of Master Black Belt can be assumed by any of the available black belts.

Important Note: Although the naming of the tanks are taken from martial arts, they do not come with the notion of Seniority in Lean Six Sigma. Nobody is nobody's "senpai" (senior) or "kouhai" (junior) in Lean Six Sigma. As such, you cannot use an LSS title to pull rank with your team (not that it is advisable to do so in recent years, mind you).

What the organizational structure simply implies is that the workload for implementing the Lean Six Sigma methodology is evenly distributed across the chart. No one is supposed to do less or more than what they were trained to do but each must make sure that they contribute to the initiative to the best of their abilities.

And, as was stated, you don't have to use this particular organizational structure for your group. Just make sure that everyone has a workload that reflects their skills and expertise while laying out a clear line of communication. This way, your team can know who reports to who and what tasks they must focus on for every phase of the project.

Tools and Techniques

Now that you know of the organizational structure of a Lean Six Sigma team, it's time to look at the tools and techniques that you are going to equip them with. A lot of these tools are older than even Lean or Six Sigma, having only been incorporated to Lean Six Sigma as the years went on.

One of the best features of Lean Six Sigma is that you don't have to master all of these tools at once. They are divided into phases meaning they only come necessary at certain points of the business process. This means that any team can pick and choose which tools to use depending on the situation. In fact, every organization has their own set of favorite tools and techniques under the Lean Six Sigma method.

But, all the same, it's time to get acquainted with you and your team's Lean Six Sigma arsenal.

1) Process Analysis

These tools are mostly associated with the Lean portion of the method. As such, they are meant to describe the process for you while also identifying what could make it efficient.

- **The Process Map** – This is a graphical display that shows how each step and process correlate with one another. In turn, this gives your team an idea as to how one decision you'd make for one part of the process would affect the rest. Each process and step will be marked as a separate item on the map.
- **Value Stream Map** –. This process map shows the primary flow of processes if every step goes as planned. A major focus here is how value is created and delivered in every part of the process.
- **As-Is Process** - This is a special variant of the process map that shows all the steps of the process as they are carried out in the business's current environment. This is not something that is exactly similar as what is documented in procedural charts.
- **To-Be Process** – If the As-Is chart shows how things are done currently, then the To-Be process shows how things are supposed to be done. This is often reflected in the revisions of the business process and its documentation that is released as part of the implementation.

- **Data Boxes** – These are located in the process and value stream maps. They are used to record the metrics associated with a particular step such as cycle times, inventory, available resources, and value-added time.

- **TAKT Time** – This is a measure that is associated with the process being analyzed. It will reflect the amount of time allowed for each process that ensures that the process meets the demands of the customer.

- **Roll Throughput Yield** – This is an equation that determines the probability that an item will pass through every part of the process properly and creates something valuable. It is done by multiplying all the step yield values from the value stream map.

- **Work-cells** – This process structure is used to speed up the flow through the process. All process steps will be arranged together in a single work cell which reduces time spent in transitioning between steps.

- **Kanban** – A variant of the lean method, Kanban is a visual scheduling approach where the previous step provides a signal for the next step to commence. On paper, this allows your team to minimize on inventory as you only have to stock up on materials necessary for that step of the project.

- **Visual Control** – This is a signaling system which allows operators to anticipate potential bottlenecks in the process. Once identified, they can then set up activities meant to relieve pressure in those areas, preventing the bottleneck from happening. It is an ideal tool for real-time process management.

2) Visual Analysis

A staple in every problem-solving methodology, visual analysis tools and techniques can be used in multiple phases in the process. And because they are visual by design, these tools are easy to understand.

They also make communicating ideas and proposals to senior management and operations easy to understand, especially in helping them see how one change can affect the solution and the process.

- **Histogram** – A vertical bar chart, this Histogram shows the relative size of different categories of various instances and occurrences. It is used for the identification of the biggest contributing attributes to a problem.

- **Pareto Chart** – This is a variant of the Histogram which organizes the biggest categories first down to the smallest. You may use this to determine which categories need to be prioritized when solving a problem.

- **Fishbone Diagram** – Also known as the Cause and Effect Program, this graph shows all the possible consequences that could occur because of an unsolved problem. This can be used as a tool to identify what caused a problem in the first place.
- **Scatter Diagram** – This chart plots two attributes that are associated in a data point. One attribute is shown on the vertical axis and the other on the horizontal axis. The diagram will show if there is a correlation or a tendency towards correlation between the two attributes.
- **Box Plots** – This tool shows the spread of data for a parameter and the nature of any attribute that tends to occur. The center half are shown in a box with a line going to value in the midpoint. The outer half of the data will then be placed in the upper and lower portions of the box, showing the extremes of what is most or least likely to occur if the attributes in the center are present.
- **Run Chart** – This diagram shows a sequence of values for a certain parameter used in a process. The values are either seen in each successive product or collected at set times in the middle of a production process.

- **Pie Chart** – This circular chart shows the relative size of categories in relation to a specific parameter. Each category gets a slice of the "pie", the ones with the heaviest correlation to a parameter getting the biggest slices.
- **Check Sheet** – A rather simple visual took, the check sheet only shows what needs to be measured in the end product. If the product meets a certain quality, that item will be marked with a check mark.
- **Solution Selection Matrix** – This matrix compares various options of a solution across several criteria. It takes inspiration from the Pugh Concept Matrix and assigns scores to each option, giving you and your team an idea as to which ones are the most applicable for a certain problem. Of course, the one that scores the highest will be the most applicable.
- **Quality Selection Matrix** – This is a matrix is a diagram that shows how the expectations and needs of the customer is met across the business process. You should use this to set performance goals for the process, identify potential waste, and any missed opportunity your team did not notice in the previous cycles.
- **Bottlenecks** – When tasks or processes start to get backed up in a part of the production cycle, this is

what is called as a bottleneck. And it is at bottlenecks where the most waste is being generated including slow moving inventory, long wait times, and extra management needed just to decongest everything.

- **Five S** – This is a special set of workplace disciplines that focus on organizing assets and resources. How your team can abide by the 5 S rules (if you apply them, of course) will determine how smooth your operations will be.
- **Poka Yoke** – If Five S is about maximizing space and wise inventory management, Poka Yoke is all about making the workplace error-proof. Used in the design process, Poka Yoke uses quality checks and gates to ensure that there are no mistakes made for every segment of the process. Or, at the very least, Poka Yoke makes mistakes even more obvious that they are now easier to address before the product gets shipped.

3) Statistical Analysis

If the analytical tools lean more to the Lean side of things, the Statistical Analysis tools would lean more to the Six Sigma side of the method. Statistical analysis helps you and your team make sense of the data that you gathered and determine what is the most significant in addressing a problem.

For these tools, you might have to purchase software such as the Excess Analysis Tool Pak or the Minitab application since processing and interpreting the data they collect manually is nothing short of difficult. Of course, the people assigned to interpret the data in these tools must be trained to do so. This means that the tools as mentioned below are something that only green belts and higher can appreciate.

- **Process Capability** – This statistical ratio compares normal process variability with the specifications set by the customer. It is expressed through metrics like Cp, Pp, Cpk, Ppk, and other variables. In short, this tool is ideal for predicting whether or not a process has the ability to deliver on the specifications without creating defects.
- **Descriptive Statistics** – These set of statistical techniques describe a normal behavior for a process in relation with a specific parameter or the end product. This includes the median, mean, mode, and standard deviation.
- **Inferential Statistics** – This statistical method is used to relate the statistical performance of a sample to the statistical performance of the larger population. This approach is reliant on the sampling

approach used and the confidence interval and level employed.

- **Measurement System Analysis** – This comprehensive analysis tool is used to inspect and test systems in their ability to correctly identify a measured value within a process or the product itself. It will include assessing the accuracy, precision, stability, linearity, and discrimination.
- **Gage R&R** – This tool is focused on determining how accurate your measurement systems being used are. It uses experiments that focus on comparing products and processes with a predetermined set of values and testing how frequently those values are being met in every production cycle.
- **Hypothesis Test** – This test is used to determine whether an assumption you set for a specific data can be verified or not. Typically, it is used in the Lean Six Sigma procedure to determine if the samples gathered are statistically similar to one another or there are substantial differences in each.

In case of dissimilarity, this would tell you and your staff that a change that you are planning to maintain can have a significant impact to the process or the end product. There are different sub-techniques that you can use here depending on the data and the number of parameters that have to be scrutinized.

4) Project and Team Management Tools

The ability to connect a project with the strategies of upper management and customers is also something that Lean Six Sigma also focuses on. Fortunately for you, there are tools and techniques that can help you manage the project and team in relation with external people.

Some of these tools are useful in understanding how external people view the project. Others are highly effective in streamlining the internal and external channels of communications. Either way, these tools can make handling your project marginally easier.

- **Critical to Quality** – These parameters focus on the product, process, and service especially on their ability to deliver on the value promised to customers. The CTQ attributes, however, is not something that you and your team would come up with. It is something that only external people like the stakeholders and the client can create for the team.
- **Project Charter** – This document is used to authorize the project and provide its scope. In

essence, they give the direction and boundaries that a team needs in order to meet the specifications of the project. There is no proper format for the charter which means organizations use their own unique framework for this.

- **In-Frame/Out-Frame** – This technique is used to clarify boundaries for a project that the team must follow. As such, the scope will be determined in this frame as well as the areas that the team must not focus on during each phase.
- **SIPOC** – This stands for Supplier, Input, Process, Output, and Customer. It is another limit-identifying technique to define the limits of the process while also helping stakeholders understand how the project can be completed.
- **The Cross-Functional Team** - This simply refers to the Six Sigma Team that you have built up regardless of its composition and set of shared responsibilities. Normally, every function of the team will have a representative who will join in on team meetings and explain key issues in their subject matter of expertise.
- **Team Decision Making** - This decentralized form of decision making puts more focus on the team coming to a consensus first before acting. Although

your teams still rely on hard data, they still have the ability to prioritize what needs to be done and who will be in charge for each segment of the implementation process.

- **Culture Change Management** - Implementing Lean Six Sigma on your projects is not going to be sustainable if you don't set up the proper support for it. This is where Culture Change Management comes in as it helps the rest of the organization get used to the new standards and master the new protocols for the business process.

A core focus in this management strategy is in building enough support during the Improvement and Control Phases. If done right, any change you would want to implement is not only effective but also sustained for a long period of time.

- **Stakeholder Management** - This is what you should use in identifying the key stakeholders in your Lean Six Sigma projects. Who are the stakeholders for each LSS project you would take? What are their performance goals and communication lines?
- **Implementation Planning** - This is a set of practices that will help the team understand how to execute a change in the project or a project itself.

Matters such as the division of labor as well as the time period for which changes should be observed will be discussed here.

To Summarize

As was previously stated, you don't have to use all of these tools for your Lean Six Sigma projects. In fact, you might have noticed that there are some tools and strategies whose goals and functions are already covered by others or that some strategies are best used for smaller or larger projects, depending on the case.

With that being said, however, there are also tools and strategies listed above that form the core concept of Lean Six Sigma. Things like setting up a Cross-Functional Team or several analytical/statistical practices are things that you and your team must set up properly in order to carry out the LSS changes in your organization.

It's up to the team, then, to determine which tools and strategies are best for their current project. It would also help the teams if they do not become dead-set on using one particular strategy over and over throughout multiple projects. It's a good thing to master a tool but this should never be done at the expense of other items in the arsenal, especially if one tool or strategy answers an issue more efficiently than the others.

Chapter 6 The Lean Six Sigma Process

The process for problem-solving under the Lean Six Sigma methodology actually borrows from its Six Sigma predecessor. In short, the process is divided into 5 phases known collectively as DMAIC or Define, Measure, Analyze, Improve, and Control.

Each of the phases has a premise or question that must be answered. And if that question is answered, the project can proceed to the next phase.

So, how long should each phase last? That depends truly on what your project is trying to solve. Normally, at the end of each phase, there is a review to discuss what has been achieved so far and what must be improved before the next phase begins.

Now, let's take a look at these phases in detail.

Define

This is the first phase of the process and must answer this question "has the problem been identified from multiple perspectives?". Normally, in this phase, a Green Belt or

Black Belt will be tasked with describing the problem to the rest of the team.

Aside from explaining the problem, the specifications for the project can also be identified. Thus, the number of yellow belts can be proposed by the team to the higher ups here as well as the scope of the entire process.

During this phase, those who will become yellow belts will have to undergo basic Lean Six Sigma training if there are no available yellow belts within the organization yet. The phase will then end with the team coming up with a project charter which identifies the problem and how the project is going to solve it. Of course, what goals must be achieved and how success will be determined may also be discussed in this phase.

Measure

In this phase, the baseline condition of the process is set up. This can be done by identifying the current performance of the progress, the product, or the service in relation to the critical attributes of quality or success as identified in the Define phase.

And what should be asked in this phase? It is "How much do we understand of the current process and can we gauge performance in each step?"

And this is where things get tricky. If you were not the one to document or even properly control every step of the process, this phase is going to take a while to complete. The reason for such is because you have to establish the current standards first so you could find out how to make improvements. And you cannot do this without documenting each step and measure of the current workflow.

The processes must be defined so that you and your team can determine the flow of one step to another especially in delivering that value until it reaches the customer.

More often than not, businesses do not have the appropriate system to measure and collect data, so they need to be developed first. This is where the subject matter experts (the green and yellow belts) will come in as they gather and interpret data from the business's current layout.

By the end of this phase, every problem and issue identified must be quantified or supported with hard data. But, most importantly, the "As-Is" state of the business process must be established so the "To-Be" Process can start to take form.

Analyze

This phase of the process is particularly focused on answering the question "What is the root cause of this problem?". In this part, every data gathered in the succeeding phases will be processed, analyzed, and interpreted by the green and black belts. As such, it is at this phase where the leader has to decide what kind of analytical and statistical tools they have to employ to determine what makes a problem tick.

It is at this phase where the concept of Hypothesis Testing comes into play. What is this, you may ask? The term might sound technical and scientific (and it is), the premise is rather simple.

When confronted with a problem, anybody of sound mind would usually come up with a theory on what caused it. Let's say, for example, that your business just had to recall batches of the products it shipped. As someone who has an understanding of the business process, you might have some hunches as to what caused it.

With your hypotheses as your base, you and your team will then conduct a series of analytical and statistical interpretation sessions to see if the data supports any of the causes you suspect produced the problem. And if not, the process will get your team acquainted with a bigger, underlying problem that has never been addressed before.

And don't worry about the math. The computations are rigorous but the process itself of comparing and contrasting data is rather straightforward. This is quite true if you and your team decide to use some tools like Excel's Analysis Tools.

Another important aspect of this phase is the accuracy of the problem you have identified. In essence, the team must be extra careful not to prepare a detailed problem statement. There is a strong chance that you might base your entire analysis on a wrongly assumed problem. This causes you to lose time and effort especially on the next phase.

Improve

It's important to remember that this is the 4th phase. Why? A lot of Lean Six Sigma teams make the mistake of rushing to this part of the process without thoroughly completing the previous three. And if your team does that, you create a solution that addresses what is merely a symptom, not the actual problem.

And thus, the question to be asked here is "Is there a solution for this problem that is viable, effective, and easy to implement?" Depending on the nature of the problem, your team members might have to assume a larger or smaller role to create a solution.

And, of course, this is going to be the more labor-extensive and expensive phase of the Lean Six Sigma process. This is where to the "To-Be" state of the process will be realized, after all, and that would involve changing equipment, adding new software, overhauling the entire production process, and re-training operators.

While implementation is on-going, the green and yellow belts do not stop in gathering and interpreting data. At this point, however, their focus is not on validating the problem but monitoring if the solution is effective in addressing a problem even at a controlled environment.

Either way, every viable solution must be thoroughly tested while the implementation materials are being developed. At the end of this phase, you and your team should have a solution ready for deployment.

Control

This is the final phase of the process and should answer the question "Can the solution now become the new standard?" To be more specific about it, the Lean Six Sigma team at this point should determine whether or not the solution has properly addressed the problem.

And not only should the solution address the issue properly, it must do so consecutively. A mistake that teams often make at this point is celebrating "false" successes where some effect they think is good occurs and they assume that this solved the problem.

All members of the project are to be involved in this phase especially in monitoring the implementation process in their respective departments. This phase will continue to remain in effect until a sense of stability can be observed. As such, this phase will take weeks to a month to occur.

In order to properly execute this phase, the team must have set up a control plan to monitor changes in the product or process. This will include thresholds wherein performance can be measured as well as corrective strategies to be implemented in case performance takes a dip.

This is a rather crucial part of the phase as the last thing you would want to happen is if everybody reverts back to the old process. In most cases, a plan of this type will also use statistical process controls.

Once the operators of the process no longer need the control and support of the project team, then and only then can you say that this phase is finished, and the entire Lean Six Sigma process is completed.

Phase Gate Reviews

So far, the Lean Six Sigma process will involve everyone in the project team and that includes the yellow, green, black, and master black belts. But they are not the only people that needs to do something in order to implement Lean Six Sigma properly.

Upper management and stakeholders also need to be aware of whatever is happening through the five phases. These people along with the master black belt, or any of available black belts, will conduct what is called as a Phase Gate Review.

So, what's a Phase Gate? It is simply that period of the process where one phase is about to end, and another begins. To be simpler about it, a Phase Gate Is that period in between phases. As such, a Phase Gate Review is simply a periodical reporting session where the team and the upper management discuss what has been achieved so far in the Lean Six Sigma methodology.

The review of Phase Gates is meant to achieve three purposes:

- Review the work of most recent phase completed to make sure that everything was done according to the LSS method. If anything, inadequate was discovered, the upper management may compel the project team to do over certain steps and come boack for another review. It is here that the Black Belt will inform the team what was their perceived weaknesses or mistakes and will coach them on how to do address such.

- Take a look at whether or not the pertinent question of the phase has been sufficiently answered. Also, the review will cover any documentation and supporting data gathered. If the data does not support the answer, the team can be compelled to continue on the phase until the question has been sufficiently answered.
- Set up the boundaries for the project. This focuses on the specifications for the next phase based on the results of the previous phase. Some examples of a boundary include setting up a time-window for data gathering and interpretation of the Measure Phase or setting up a budget limit for implementations in the Improve Phase.

One Important Note: Of course, it is assumed that the people doing the Phase Gate Review are aware of the basics of the Lean Six Sigma process. After all, nothing can derail and demoralize a project more than a committee that asks the wrong questions for any given phase.

For instance, if the upper management persists on making the team find a solution for a problem when everybody is still in the Define Phase is a bit premature. The proper forum for that question is for the Phase Gate review for the Analyze Phase.

As such, it is the duty of the assigned Black Belt to make sure that the reviewing team are aware of what questions the team is trying to answer for each phase of the process. This includes cutting them promptly (politely, of course. Remember that they are still your superiors) and informing that such question should be reserved later.

And, of course, you should be ready for the possibility for resistance of miscommunication in this part of the process. Thus, you should find a way to make sure that everybody in the team and the higher ups are in the same page.

If your team has a concern that they need to be addressed or a special request for the next phase, they must not feel intimidated by the higher ups to ask for assistance in such. And if the higher ups feel that the project is getting out of hand, you must find a way to communicate the same without demoralizing your team.

An open and transparent line of communication will actually help you bridge the gap between your teams and the higher-ups that all of you have to answer to in the end. And if both parties are satisfied, any favorable response you get from either is a tell-tale sign that everybody has understood the important of the Lean Six Sigma initiative.

Chapter 7 Lean Six Sigma in Action

So, how do you go about applying the Lean Six Sigma Process?

This is a rather loaded question because the methodology is not something that is actually that easy to comprehend, especially if you are new to it. And talking about this methodology using complex, technical words without some illustration is not going to help matters.

But, don't worry. It is a rather straightforward process which is why it is best to discuss each phase of the methodology by using a real-world scenario.

The Problem

For the rest of the chapter, you and I are going to solve a problem that maybe hypothetical but is based on what is currently happening in various homes across the world. In fact, you might have encountered this yourself.

Every morning when you go out for work, what is the one thing that you always do aside from taking a bath and taking in your morning coffee?

If you answered, "look for my keys", then you and perhaps millions of other readers are correct. And here lies the problem: What if you can't find them quickly?

You rummage through the pants you've used last night, and they weren't there. You checked the countertop and it they aren't there. You check the hook where you usually hang them, and they aren't there. Now, you're getting frustrated. Let us say, for brevity's sake, that you found them at the couch to your immediate relief.

The question now is this: how many minutes every day that did you lose over finding your keys? How many times in a week were you at risk of missing the bus or train to the city? And, what if you arrive at your business only to find out that you brought the WRONG set of keys which means you can't unlock important storage units and containers until someone who has the duplicates does it for you?

The point is that this mild annoyance has occurred multiple times in the past and has been affecting how you start your day. And, you being the responsible kind of person, decided that enough is enough and would want to put up something that makes sure that this does not ever happen again.

Now, it is time to apply the Lean Six Sigma Methodology to solve this problem of yours.

A. Define Phase

First, let's start by considering this problem from the perspective of the customer. So, who's the person going to benefit greatly from your changes? Yes, that's right. You.

How are you going to benefit from this? For starters, you now have a definite place to store your keys every night. This means you cut down on time looking for them which means you don't leave your home in a hurry.

Next, there is the fact that you always have the right set of keys with you. Whether you are opening the business or a more personal storage container, you always have the right key for every lock that you encounter for a single day.

Either way, the keys can be in one place that you can immediately head out and pick up every morning. Based upon the In-Frame and Out-of-Frame, you can decide to limit the process to what you do with the keys every night and at morning of the next day. You will not include everything else that does not involve your fingers touching those keys such as taking a bath or eating your breakfast.

Thus, the goal of your project in the charter is to implement a system where you can immediately acquire the right set of keys before you head out of the house.

B. Measure Phase

At this phase, you should start creating a process map that shows what could possible happen to your keys from the moment you arrive at home and ends with your arrival at the office the next day. This process can have different branches depending on whether the following day is a regular workday, a weekend, or a holiday.

You can even differentiate things further to accommodate variables like you going out the night before or the weather was bad that you required additional preparation time the next morning. You might even have to factor in every unplanned shift in your usual activities like having to work overtime or encountering an emergency on the road.

Either way, you will find out that mapping the process for weekends and holidays are so varied that it is next to impossible. But the process for your weekdays can be predictable which makes mapping easy.

Your As-Is process may look something like this:

1. Arrive at home
2. Unlock Door
3. Put things on desk
4. Empty pocket
5. Change clothes
6. (Evening passes and morning comes)
7. Get dressed
8. Grab things on desk

9. Find your keys

10. Lock the door

11. Arrive at work

12. Unlock desk, cabinets, and other storage units

You can even add time metric and success metric for each step. Just keep in mind, however, that there are only three of those steps that have a value-added time element to them. Those steps are emptying pockets, finding the keys, and unlocking the doors and cabinets. And, of course, all of those steps have a high success metric except for Finding the Keys.

One challenge you will face in mapping the process is defining a pass or fail condition for each step. This can be obvious as you have to determine the purpose of each step to identify what outcome you desire the most.

You then have to collect data for these steps in a span of four weeks or more. You check sheets every night before bedtime and take notes of how much time each step must be completed. At the same time, you record everything that you have done with your keys if ever there you have to use them on a weekend or a holiday during that data gathering period.

One other challenge that you would have to face during this time is something called the Hawthorne Effect. This is where the measurement of a parameter changes what people do. Simply put, since you are now monitoring what you are doing, you subconsciously change your behavior to become more cautious.

It's similar to how wait staff behave if they know one of the diners in the evening happens to be a Michelin reviewer. If the subjects know that they are being measured, their behavior changes to respond to the test.

As such, you run the risk of not collecting data that would reflect your usual daily performance under the process. In this scenario, your brain might subconsciously remember where you left your keys, impacting the results in step 9.

C. Analyze Phase

Now that you have data, you can start analyzing your process. Sure, there is no data for weekends and holidays but the lack of such provides little variation for the process most of the time. The point is that you know have a sequence of events that depict what happens to your keys the moment you arrive at home and when you arrive for work the next; and backed up by hard data.

So, you create a Fishbone Diagram to determine the root causes. Perhaps you came up with six possible causes given your regular proximity to the place where you should place the keys every night or how active you are outside of work.

So, your diagram could look something like this:

Drops Keys No proper key placement Keys get stuck in couch

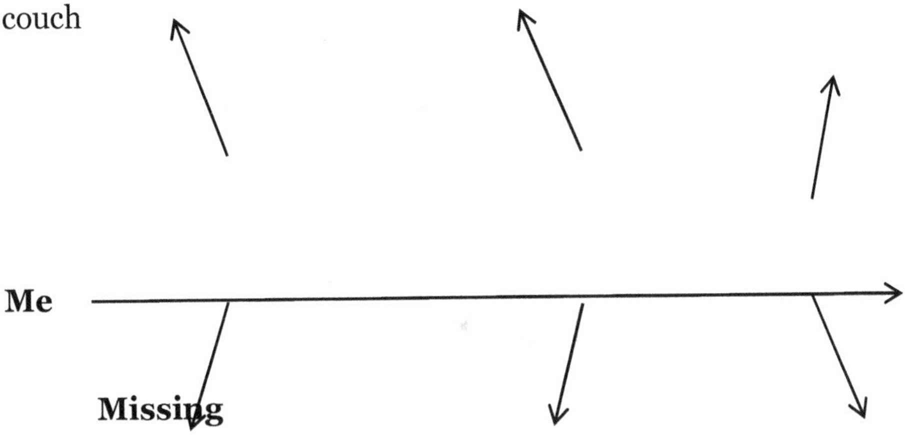

Keys

Got drunk last night Increment weather Housemates move them

Your Fishbone diagram can also be explained like this:

a) You don't have a designated place to store your keys at every night.

b) You just drop the keys wherever you place your baggage at.

c) You drop the keys right at your last known spike of activity I.e. the couch after binge-watching your favorite show.

d) In days when the weather is bad, where you have extra layers of clothing, you just place your keys at the pocket of your coat which hangs at the closet.

e) You have nightly drinking sessions with your friends which causes you to black out and not remember where you placed your keys in the morning after.

f) When someone you live with sees that your keys are placed in an unusual location, they might move it without asking your permission.

Now, which of these possible causes are most likely to occur? You can arrange the causes according to their order of possibility and frequency which might look like this:

1. No proper key placement

2. Drops Keys

3. Keys stuck in couch

4. Housemates move them

5. Increment weather

6. Got drunk

So, you can figure out that a lack of key placement is the most frequently-occurring possible root cause of your problem. But you think for yourself "Does it share elements with the rest?". You might be surprised that possible causes that share a common element might point you to the presence of a bigger, underlying issue. Let's take a look.

If you have a tendency to just drop your keys wherever you left your bags, that means that your brain does not recognize a system where you should place key items of your work at home. And if your keys do get left in the coach after your last nighttime activity, that also points to the fact that you don't have a set system for key placement.

If your housemates tend to relocate your keys, that means that there is no set system for proper key placement at home. And if you lose your keys because you blacked out last night, then your brain does not subconsciously recognize where to place the keys even at an inebriated state.

So, what do these possible causes share? Yes, that's right. You do not have a definite place where the keys can be stored every time you arrive at home.

If you want to be detailed about it, your analysis could look like this:

Problem: You take time finding your keys every morning.

Primary Cause: When arriving at home, you just place the keys wherever you feel like it. Sometimes, it just stays in your coat or back pocket hours after arrival.

Root Cause: No defined system for proper key placement established at home.

D. Improve Phase

This is now the time to come up with a solution. The question, however, is this: which solution is the best? There are many ways to address your key problem. Your first option was to put a lock on the door so that you can just place the keys there. But the strategy is not particularly good to look at and the hook is too small that you might end up forgetting it existed in the first place.

The next option is to connect your keys to your bag or belt. However, the connecting chains are too gaudy to look at and you run the risk of losing your keys if you lose your belt or bag. The third option was to place an RFID tag on your keys which can be monitored via an app. Your only concern here is that the RFID system is more expensive.

You could weigh the pros and cons of each but that is not exactly methodical as the Lean Six Sigma framework requires you to be. At this point, you can use a Solution Selection Matrix where each solution will be graded in several categories

Let us say that an option that gets a perfect score in one category should get 5 points and the lowest possible score is 1. So here's an example:

Solution	**Low Cost**	**Aesthetics**	**Convenience**	**Total**
Door Hook	4	2	5	11
RFID	1	5	5	11
Belt/Bag Chain	3	1	3	7
A bowl on the desk	5	5	5	15
Get a duplicate	2	3	5	10

At a glance, you noticed that the Bowl on Desk solution ranked the highest. Why? It is cheap to acquire, it blends well with your current table/counter layout, and it is big enough to be noticed whenever you enter the room.

And thus, you decided to use the Bowl on Desk strategy to address the issue. Now, how should it be incorporated to your process? It might look something like this:

1. Arrive home

2. Unlock Door

3. Put things on desk

4. Empty pocket

5. Place keys on bowl

6. Change clothes

7. Check keys if they are on the bowl before going to sleep

8. (Evening passes and morning comes)

9. Get dressed

10. Grab things on desk

11. Get keys from bowl

12. Lock the door

13. Arrive at work

14. Unlock desk, cabinets, and other storage units

And because the bowl is placed on the desk, it itself can serve as a Poka Yoke reminder of your key's status. Simply put, if the key is not there, it should be in the pocket of your coat or pants. Also, this solution addresses five out of six problems found in the measure phase.

There is now a process defined for every day of the week, including the weekends and holidays. You could even add another Poka Yoke to the solution like making sure that the keys are always placed in the same pocket regardless of whatever you are wearing. Or you could add an item like a tag to differentiate this set of keys from the others. This way, you don't mistakenly bring the wrong set of keys at work.

You might have noticed that we didn't take away any crucial step in the process but added more. Whether or not this would benefit the overall process would be seen in the next phase.

E. Control Phase

Since this problem did not require a cross-functional team, this phase should be easy to complete. To do this, monitor any change that has occurred in your process. Did you leave your home on time? Did you arrive at work with a calmer state of mind?

And as for the application of the process, were the new steps easy to achieve and maintain? Were you placing the keys at the bowl every night and then remembering to immediately go there before leaving work?

You need to monitor the process to make sure that it works, and this is where a control plan will come into play.

First, set up a response plan where you and your housemates would look for the keys if they are not on the bowl before bedtime. Second, you should also set up fail safes in case the process cannot be followed due to extraordinary circumstances.

For instance, you are about to go out for another drinking party with your friends. Knowing that you tend to black out and forget what you did last night, you might want to set up a system where your friend designated to be the most sober (or least drunk) of that night would place the key in the bowl. This way, you can be assured that your items are still in place even if you are trying to remember what happened to you last night.

Or you just don't get too drunk to the point of passing out. That works, too.

After three weeks if the solution is maintained, you can then be certain that the problem has been eliminated. And although the new process has 3 more steps which you think would defeat the purpose of the Lean system, it actually removed a huge portion of your time looking for the keys every morning.

With search times drastically reduced, overall efficiency in the process was increased and the margin of error was also dropped to non-existent levels. Customer satisfaction is guaranteed, and you could go about your day not worrying what will happen to your keys in the next morning.

The Takeaway

This is but one of the simpler applications of Lean Six Sigma. Of course, large business projects will require more steps and will most definitely go through a lot of processes, key issues, and collaborations across cross-functional teams. In fact, we did not do any Phase Gate review in this scenario since it was so simple and minor in scope.

The point is that the Lean Six Sigma methodology always follows the same straightforward sequence. It begins with you identifying a problem and ends with you making a solution sustainable.

Now, does that mean that every solution that you and your team discovered through Lean Six Sigma be really effective in the long term. The answer, sadly, is no. There are chances when your solution becomes too unmanageable and this could be caused by factors outside of your control.

A policy-based solution, for example, can be delayed by corporate politics and bureaucracy that its effects can get diminished the longer the solution is applied. A technology-based solution, on the other hand, can be rendered obsolete if a new system is introduced in the market mid-implementation.

What could this mean for you? It only tells you that you must do the Lean Six Sigma process again. Identify a key issue, find the latest solutions, and implement those before everything becomes too late.

Of course, you can also do things that take the concept of the Lean Six Sigma even further and come up with a system that is effective and sustainable for your organization. This will include addressing some key issues inherent with Lean Six Sigma itself.

Chapter 8 The Art of Decluttering

The core premise of Lean Six Sigma is the streamlining of your business processes. As such, it is important that you also deal with something that has plagued many businesses and private individuals in order to apply the Lean Six Sigma methodology. After all, the method is just as effective as the team and operator using it.

And thus, it is best that we have to confront one of business's dirtiest words: Clutter. Heck, even the way it rolls of the tongue sounds offensive.

It has been a fodder for reality TV shows like Hoarders and, on a business perspective, a bad business model regardless of your process methodology.

Of course, the remedy here is to un-clutter but that does pose a question:

"How Do I Do It?"

To answer that question, let us start with the ABCs.

Why Get Rid of Clutter?

It is easy to talk about decluttering but why should you it? There are various legitimate reasons why you should make certain aspects of your business and personal operations less of a mess, particularly:

- **Space**

Basically, clutter takes up space that could have been used for more useful ventures. For instance, look at an LSS-optimized storage facility and one that is, well, not LSS-optimized.

The former may be filled with a lot of things, depending on the project, but you can be certain that every item stored there has a purpose relative to the phase of the project. The latter, on the other hand, is not only filled with a lot of things but 99% of these things cannot be used for any immediate reason.

Which of the two is maximizing the available space? Naturally, not the cluttered one.

And apart from taking up physical space, the clutter also tends to take over everybody's mind. The more clutter, the more things you and your team will have to maintain in a functional state in the hope that they'd be useful sometime in the future.

- **Prioritization**

Going back to hoarding, why do you think that hoarders can't get rid of what they own? They believe that these things are highly valuable, despite having greatly depreciated. Alternatively, they think that these objects might become important for some undetermined purpose for an undetermined future.

Simply put, everything is precious in a room which is why nothing should be thrown away – this is how clutter takes form.

The Lean Six Sigma method requires you to be as objective as possible, seeing the real importance of the things that you should keep over the things you think you should keep. Eventually, this can be applied in mental clutter, with which you and your team start prioritizing activities and steps that add value to the end product.

It is not practical to keep on doing things that don't contribute to work productivity.

- **Cost Effectiveness**

It goes without saying that you eventually spend less if you have need of less things in your business. But, even if you argue that the things that you acquired were cheap in the first place, maintaining them or sorting through them does cost you a pretty penny in the long run. You have to remember that the price of any item is not just limited to the one listed on the price tag.

Let's say that you bought a secondhand printer for your business which cost you $30.00. A printer nowadays will cost $60.00 at the very least. But the cheap printer malfunctions twice a month, it skips lines when printing, or the ink bleeds out of the canisters from time to time. So, adding the constant maintenance costs and the occasional expletive that your staff utters when using the printer, did you save on $30.00 or did you waste $30.00 or more instead?

This is the same thing that happens if you purchase unnecessary assets to your business. Do they need regular repairs and maintenance? Can you move them on your own or do you have to hire people to transport them? These kinds of operational cost make clutter expensive, eventually.

- **Profit**

This may be the most direct result of cleaning up your storage area in terms of the financial aspect. Take advantage of their value by simply transferring ownership to others. By selling items that you don't have a need of gives you profit – allowing you to declutter and earn a little. Your loss could be someone's gain. To make it easier for you, just think that you are simply giving others a chance to enjoy the things you used to be fond of.

“But is LSS about throwing away waste? Who’s going to find my useless stuff valuable? You ask. The truth with the Lean Six Sigma method is that it deals with waste that personally hinders you from becoming efficient in your operations. If we were to make that simpler, it helps you deal with YOUR waste, the elements or byproducts of your actions that do not bring value but might be valuable to someone else.

And speaking of value, there is a huge possibility that you might discover the real value of the things that are taking up your physical space which may be higher than your perceived value over them. If you’ve caught an episode of the TV program, Pawn Stars, there are instances when the real value of an item considered by others to be trash, is made known – where an expert confirms a particular item is worth thousands of dollars.

That deck of trading cards collecting dust in your attic might be a collector’s item. That piece of clothing that almost looks like a rag could be a relic from 100 years into the past. That thingamabob with some weird scribbles? A movie prop signed by a famous actor. And so on and so forth.

Sure, the pawnshop would do their best to give a low estimate but the sheer surprise as to knowing how valuable that thing is for somebody else is always entertaining to watch.

On a business setting, such instances are hard to find. That piece of equipment that is rusting in your storage areas might not even come up to a quarter of their original price. But let us just say that you are better off earning a few dollars by selling these things as opposed to them taking up useful space in your business.

- **It Helps you Comply with Lean Six Sigma**

Naturally, decluttering your physical space is compatible with your Lean Six Sigma Goals. Keep in mind that decluttering is more than just getting rid of everything useless that is taking up space in the room. It is also about arranging the layout of the room so that space is maximize and no movement is wasted being there.

For example, if you want the front desk moved so that your secretary has a better sight of people entering the door, that move is easier if there are fewer, unused tables or other fixtures standing in the way. Or what if a stack of magazines is starting to form in one side of the area and next to a naked power outlet? That's an obvious fire hazard right there for you and your staff.

By decluttering the place, you open up the area to be redesigned into whatever you want. Applying this with the Lean Six Sigma, you give your business the physical and mental reordering it needs to embrace the methodology better.

- **Decluttering the Right Way**

Getting rid of excessive items that you may have accumulated over the years can be quite challenging. Here are a few helpful tips to get you started:

A. For Physical Spaces

1. One at a Time

The biggest hurdle you'll have to face would be losing interest during the process of decluttering. For one, if you have acquired too many items, you are likely to go the easy way out – abandoning the task. The one big challenge in decluttering is

To make this less of a challenge for you, you and your staff should commit to identifying 1 item each that needs to go for that day. If your project team is made up of 10 people and there are hundreds of items to be disposed of, then you can create a system wherein your team will deal with them one at a time.

You don't need to get rid of them all at the same time, take it step-by-step. Remember it's a process, there is no shortcut to it. It may appear to be a slow process, but things can get done, rather successfully. That's more than important, and that's progress.

2. List them Down

A good way to making the cleaning initiative sustainable for your team is to provide some system for it. Firstly, divide the area into smaller sectors and list all the items which have been identified as "for disposal".

It will also help if you will also create a schedule for every area, to make decluttering more orderly and efficient. It even helps if the cleaning activity is a Lean Six Sigma project itself. That way, your decluttering drive has become part of the organizations LSS campaign.

Aside from helping you complete an inventory of the things that the business owns, listing everything down (and adding a schedule) makes it easier to identify the things that need to be kept and those that need to be discarded. You'll be surprised to find items you'll never even remember you had (or bought).

B. For People and Activities

1. Prioritize, Prioritize, Prioritize

A good strategy of taking control of the business's daily operations or your own activities is to create a to-do list, ranked according to importance (or urgency). Start by writing down all the goals that the group must achieve. After that, determine if the planned activities will help you achieve these goals.

But do remember to not bind yourself to this list. The order of priority can change according to external factors. The point here is that you must always check that every move that your business makes is serving the more immediate goals and achieving long-term plans.

2. Write Things Down

This might sound cliché but having a journal of important activities can help you in a number of ways. First, it helps you de-congest your mind and organize your thoughts.

The reason why the mind gets overworked is because you let your thoughts uncontrollably pile up. Writing them down helps you pause and reorganize.

Second, it helps you monitor your progress. This could help in the Improve and Control phases as the subtlest of changes in behavior and performance can be noted and recorded. And nothing can be rewarding than looking back at a journal and seeing how you and your team have gradually improved over a period of time.

3. Never Multitask

A cardinal sin that business owners and managers often make is encouraging people to do many things at once. This is even made more apparent if a deadline is nearing. Soon enough, you would be pulling people from their own projects and making them work overtime.

Do not get the wrong idea, though. Multitasking is effective but only in short (and I mean really, really short) bursts of activity. If there are a lot of things to accomplish, prioritize those that need to be done immediately. You can go back to the lesser items once you're done with the urgent tasks.

However, if it composes your entire business or personal strategy, then you are likely to generate more clutter than what you started with. If possible, complete items on your to-do list one at a time.

And this is where your Lean Six Sigma tools can also play a role in. The method can help you identify key areas where bottlenecks can occur. The better you are at predicting where everyone has to deal with a lot of work backlog, the faster your team can be in preventing bottlenecks from happening.

This way, everybody in your team can finish every important task without becoming too tired for the next phase of the Lean Six Sigma project.

The 5S Methodology

Efficiency is all about doing more while using less. The Lean Six Sigma also operates in ensuring that your business is as efficient as possible.

However, there are other methodologies out there that you can use in Tandem with Lean Six Sigma. One of these efficiency-focused methods is 5S.

What is it, exactly? 5S are a set of principles that help your business maximize its available space and resources while also eliminating waste. This means that it is highly compatible with Lean Six Sigma and your decluttering initiative especially since it aims to make your workspace organized, clean, and safe.

And like Lean Six Sigma, 5S is used by many industries today in tandem with other methodologies.

Why Implement It?

Lean Six Sigma already is focused on identifying waste. So why bother with another methodology with 5S? This is because the 5S method looks at waste differently. If waste in the LSS method impedes your ability to provide value to the end product, then waste in 5S directly impedes your operations by making it unsafe to be in your workplace in the first place.

For instance, leaks and spills on the floors increase the risk of people slipping there, costing your business more money in medical expenses and insurance coverage. Another example is the presence of byproducts like crumpled paper and disused periodicals like newspaper and magazines which easily ignite when exposed to a source of fire.

Therefore, the 5S is best if implemented along with Lean Six Sigma. Although, there is no stopping you from implementing the same as a standalone method.

Implementation

Like Lean Six Sigma, 5S is divided into, well, 5 phases. They are as follows:

1. "Seiri" or Sort

At this phase, your team should go through all items in the work area. This includes tools, supplies, raw materials, components, cleaning equipment, and others. The designated 5S leader should then evaluate and review every item contained within that group and identify which ones are essential for everyday operations and which ones are not.

Every essential and unessential item will then be cataloged and tagged with set markers. Also, there might be items that are essential but are not used frequently. The 5S leader must evaluate how often these items are used to limit their amount in the work area.

2. "Seiton" or Straighten

Once every item has been identified and marked in the work area, it is now time to divide the place into "zones". These zones are where your every item must be placed in order to eliminate waste of all types.

For example, in order to eliminate waste of movement, all essential items must be within the reach of an operator. Handheld tools must be found at desks within chest-level of the person and heavier tools at their feet. The less they have to go to one place of the room to get important items, the faster they can finish their work.

And what about waste in the form of unwanted byproducts or damaged equipment? The room must have a designed red zone where these items can be placed. Of course, the red zone must be cleared of items on a weekly or daily basis.

The labels for each item must also be detailed. It must show the designation of the item, where it should be stored, and where it must be placed if it becomes damaged. The recommended quantities for each item must also be provided.

3. "Seiso" or Shine

Once everything is in place, the third step is to remove every trash in the area. This includes regular disposals of garbage as well as cleaning of regularly used equipment.

Remember that unkempt process equipment increases variability as well as equipment failure. And the more that your equipment fails, the more waste in the form of delays occur in your business process.

Also, dirt in the area increases the presence of workplace hazards which leads to injuries, or worse. To prevent any of these, your team must set up a regular cleaning procedure. If possible, the workspace must be cleaned before and after every work shift.

The 5S leader must also check the place and make sure that it is free of potential work hazards. This includes exposed electrical cables, burnt out bulbs, and oily leaks. And if they do find such, they must notify the rest of the team in order to address the issue as quickly as possible.

4. "Seiketsu" or Standardize

Perhaps the most important step, this part involves setting up standards for everyone else to follow. What signifies a clean and safe workspace? What are the types of waste that people must dispose of? How should one dispose of waste?

In this step, the leader must set up instructions, checklists, and other documents for others to peruse. This can even come in the form of company memorandums where the rest of organization can be informed of how to do the 5S process.

The goal here is to simplify the 5S process in such a way that everybody understands how to clean their own workspaces. Operators must also be trained in detecting deviations from the standard and addressing them either on their own or with others.

Scheduling is also an important aspect of this phase. You must set up regular cleaning and maintenance processes for the equipment in each area.

5. "Shitsuke" or Sustain

One of the most challenging parts of any new standard is to make the changes sustainable. After all, the chances of people slipping back to old standards and regressing are always high in any organizational initiative.

During this phase, an audit system must be put in place. The goal here is to make sure that not only has 5S been properly implemented in the workplace but has been ingrained into the overall organizational culture.

In essence, people in your organization must be implementing 5S not because a memo says so but it's they identify with it as part of the company's core values. This phase can last for more than a month as habits can form within no less than 30 days.

Additional Step: Safety

Some groups added a "+1" step in their process, making the method 5S+1. The additional step focuses on Safety, specifically in identifying potential work hazards and removing them.

This step also includes the selection of standardized equipment, tools, and workstations that were designed with ergonomics in mind. In essence, this step answers the question "is Safety being put first in the organization?".

To Summarize

It goes without saying that cleaning the physical workspace is integral to the Lean Six Sigma methodology. However, the culture itself needs to embrace the notion of cleanliness and change in order for any methodology to be sustainable there.

After all, any system will not be followed, and people will regress to old standards if you don't place any system to make sure that people would actually work according to the new status quo. As such, in a lot of cases, the culture of the organization must be addressed if you want your decluttering and cleaning efforts to count in the long run.

This means that you have to deal with how your organization defines and sees the Waste that it produces, either unintentionally or deliberately.

Chapter 9 D.O.W.N.T.I.M.E.

The Lean Six Sigma methodology has always been rather obsessed with eliminating waste. And if you are running a business that offers any tangible product or service, you are bound to generate waste whether you are aware of it or not.

In the Japanese language, the closest term you can get to waste is "Muda" and the Lean system has identified 8 types of Mudas that anybody can create in their business operations. If you are serious about optimizing your work area, you should at the very least be able to identify what these wastes are, how they are formed, and how they could leave an impact to your business.

But to make this easier for you, let's called the 8 Deadly Wastes as DOWNTIME which is fitting since you are bound to make a lot of temporary halts to your process if these issues prevail in your business. DOWNTIME simply means: Defects, Overpopulation, Waiting, Not Utilizing Talent, Transportation, Inventory Excess, Motion Waste, Excess Processing.

Defects

The most basic definition of a defect is that it is a deviation from the set standard. If, say, your production process was meant to create 82 cans of fresh tomatoes, a defect in that system would be a can filled only halfway through or tomatoes stored in a dented can.

Or, in software development, defects could manifest through glitches in the code or program-crashing bugs that were not addressed before the program was mass produced and shipped to the market. Either way, any element in the product that does not reflect the quality that you are looking for in the production process or what a client expressly states that your business should create can be labeled as a defect.

Defects can be caused by a number of reasons which include:

☐ Poor Quality Assurance Checks or None at All.

☐ Poor equipment maintenance.

☐ Lack or improper documentation of the process (No standards set).

☐ Un-optimized processes or steps of the process.

☐ Not understanding customer specifications.

☐ No control of inventory levels.

☐ Poor overall production design.

☐ Design changes improperly documented.

You may ask yourself "can defects be eliminated entirely from the process?" The answer, sadly, is no. But you can actually minimize the chances of them occurring.

Under the Six Sigma method, good odds for the appearance of defects in your production process should be 1 to 3 over 1 million. If we are going to translate that to percentages, your production success rate should be 99.9999% at best.

Overproduction

You might think that producing more than what is required is good but, on the Lean Six Sigma perspective, it's actually detrimental to your business. When your staff blindly produce, you are reducing important business capital.

For instance, if you produced 40 car windows instead of 20, how much of those 40 windows are a sure sell? 50% only. As for the rest, they'd be collecting dust in a storage area where they are going to depreciate in value. So, your production team has just wasted their time, money, and effort on 20 windows that will not be paid for by customers.

This usually occurs in manufacturing business but there is a chance that this could happen to your work area as well especially if you have been facing bottlenecks in the past. Overproduction can happen when:

☐ You implement Just-in-Case production policies.

☐ The customer specifications are not properly defined or understood.

☐ Forecast-based production cycles.

☐ Long set up times.

☐ Changes in engineering.

☐ Unoptimized automation.

The most obvious solution here is to streamline the flow of work. It must be simple enough that the customer can understand it. And if they understand it, they can rein in their expectations and give you specifications that you can attain given your current layout.

If necessary, you must also change the sequence of steps by adding new ones, replacing old ones, or removing entire steps altogether. This is important in reducing bottlenecks which should prevent your business from either under-performing or over-delivering.

Waiting

When some part of the process gets backed up, the flow of materials and other resources stops. What happens then is that the subsequent steps have to stop functioning so that the backed-up step can be cleared.

Wait times usually happens because a machine breaks down. For example, your business designs and creates books for clients. What happens, then, if your primary printers are taken out of commission because they need repairs? Your team will have nothing to do but wait until the printers are repaired or replaced.

Aside from equipment malfunctions, waiting can happen since your team is waiting for raw materials to be approved or just because your inventory of important components ran out. Other causes include:

☐ Imbalance in the workloads (others have light ones and others have heavy loads).

☐ Emergency downtime due to equipment failure.

☐ Long set up times.

☐ Forecast-based production.

☐ Too many work absences.

☐ Poor process quality.

☐ Production miscommunications.

☐ Insufficient resources.

Whatever the cause was, the most important aspect you have to address here is the bottleneck. Adequate staffing and the proper balancing of workloads can do a lot to prevent this problem from occurring in the future. Or, at the very least, you can gradually minimize its magnitude until bottlenecking becomes insignificant to your business operations.

Not Utilizing Talent

Although this is not a form of waste recognized in the older Lean framework, the improper utilization of human resources has become a major problem for companies today. As far as this waste is concerned, any company can generate it in two ways.

First, you either assign people who are not properly trained for the task. This could mean that their skills are not compatible with the specifications of the task or that the administration simply did not give them enough tools to successfully complete their jobs.

Second, you may hire people who are overqualified for the job. If you hire a professional to do menial labor, are you really making full use of their talents? You are just paying them for their raw strength which anybody can do. In essence, you may be using your assets but the way they are being utilized is not optimized.

Regardless of the situation, your business is liable for not utilizing your worker's talent in the following:

☐ Assigning the wrong people for the wrong tasks.

☐ Wasteful administrative activity like micromanaging tasks.

☐ Poor communication, if any.

☐ Lack of team cohesion and collaboration.

☐ Poor human resource management.

☐ Insufficient training.

☐ Not providing workers with workspace conducive to their personal development.

All of these problems point to one source: a lack of effective human resource management. Fortunately, the solutions are equally simple which includes proper employee training, continuous employee development, and the ability to resist to micromanage everything in the business.

Transportation

This type of waste is something that is directly tied to company logistics. Transportation waste is often seen in manufacturers since they have to manage the logistics of products and raw materials in between facilities and the marketplace. But make no mistake. Even business offices can do this with the improper transportation of documents and other forms of correspondence.

The premise of this waste is simple: Transportation is costly. The more you make motions that do not involve delivering the end product to the customer, the more money you lose.

Also, transportation significantly exposes products and raw materials to elements beyond your control that would damage them or make them deteriorate. And there have been far too many instances when products and materials get damaged at the road or on the sea for factors that may have not foreseen.

Here are some ways that can create transportation waste:

- ☐ Poor business layout.
- ☐ Excessive process steps.
- ☐ Misaligned flow of the process.
- ☐ Unoptimized production and delivery systems.

The best method to minimize on transportation waste is to simplify the process. If one thing can be done in 3 steps instead of 5, the margin for error is considerably smaller. This could also be solved by optimizing the layout of the workplace or office, limiting the transition of products from facility to market, and shortening the distances between process phases.

Inventory Excesses

A direct effect of overproducing, excesses in your inventory happen when there are more products and components to store in your storage areas, waiting when they will be useful; if ever they become useful.

Think of it this way: a client ordered only 20 items from you and yet you made 40. Why would they go out of the way to pay for 40 when you were only asked for 20? The rest will be stored somewhere else in the hope that someone will order them in the future.

And while they are waiting, they are deteriorating. Soon enough, that thing which was in pristine condition would degrade until it is of no value when somebody does order for it.

This is a problem usually seen in manufacturing businesses, but food service providers often deal with this more given that their products have shorter lifespans. For instance, if one item in the menu is not in demand, a sensible chef would not order for its ingredients frequently. Or, they ask for a reservation a week before so they could add the food items to next week's market budget.

Because if that piece of meat or fish stays in the freezer too long and nobody is ordering for a dish that needs such, it is going to spoil. In essence, spending on $3,000.00 worth of food items without an assurance that they are going to sell on the next day is the same with wasting $3,000.00 on a poorly thought-out gamble.

- ☐ Overproduction and buffers.
- ☐ Poor QA and monitoring systems.
- ☐ Uncoordinated production schedules and paces.
- ☐ Untrustworthy suppliers.
- ☐ Long set up times.
- ☐ Miscommunication with customer specifications.

Motion Waste

This is where the Non-value Adding Activities will fall under. Simply put, any activity that your team makes that does not ultimately lead to delivering value through the production process is wasteful by nature. For instance, if a request for certain raw materials takes 10 steps to complete when it could have been done in 3, then the system is unoptimized.

Or what if your staff have to walk 100 meters to a separate building, go through a requesting desk, fill out the papers, wait for 30 minutes to get the request approved, and then return to their desks?

It might sound reasonable if the item in question is large like a laptop computer but what if the item being requested were a box of staple clips or even 10 reams of bond paper? They would have saved a lot more time if everything the needed were within arm's reach.

Other Motion wastes would include:

- ☐ Poorly designed processes.
- ☐ Poor workspace layout.
- ☐ Sharing of tools and machines.
- ☐ Congested workspaces.
- ☐ Isolated operations.
- ☐ Unnecessary bureaucracy and corporate red tape.
- ☐ Lack of standards.

The most effective solution here is to re-arrange the physical layout of the work area. By decreasing the distance between workstations and other fixtures, your staff can do their work at a faster pace.

Also, giving the organization policies and systems an overhaul would come in handy here. The system wherein items requests can be checked and approved must not take more than 10 minutes to complete.

Excess Processing

If products can be overproduced, they can also be over processed. Over processing can occur when an item goes through several steps which share many similarities with one another. Or it could happen when the production process is needlessly long, filled with phases that could have otherwise been removed.

For example, are three successive quality assurance checks that necessary when the quality of the product can be determined by just one or two? Or what if a bottling process features two automated capping machines, one that would twist the cap and the other to seal it? That is an over processed production layout right there.

Other cases of excessive processing would include:

- ☐ Too much reporting or documentation.
- ☐ Excessive paperwork.
- ☐ Reentering or duplicating recorded data.
- ☐ Overdesigned production equipment.
- ☐ Human errors.

As with other production wastes, over processing can be addressed by simplifying and optimizing the production layout. This includes removing unnecessary steps or spreading multiple checks and balance functions across the entire process and not successively.

Understanding Process Variation

How about the Six Sigma part of the process? How is waste manifested and understood with this statistical method? The answer lies in something called Variation.

What is Variation, then? To answer that, you must understand that there are actually eight dimensions of quality which are:

1. Conformance
2. Performance

3. Features

4. Reliability

5. Durability

6. Serviceability

7. Aesthetics

8. Perceived Quality

Each of these dimensions are self-exclusive from one another. What this means is that customers might think that a product or service is good in terms of Reliability but would be otherwise terrible in Performance or Aesthetics.

However, some dimensions work in conjunction with each other depending on the nature of the product. If a product is Durable, then it could also be Reliable.

But, as far as Six Sigma is concerned, it focuses on the dimension of Conformance. You have to remember that customer perception is important in the Lean Six Sigma method since it is they that will ultimately determine of what you offer was actually good.

To put it in other words, quality for a customer is determined by how well it conforms to their standards, whatever those standards may be.

What is Conformance?

This is simply the degree to which something that you offer to the market meets a predefined set of standards. It is important to remember as well that your services and products offered are a function or manifestation of your internal processes as well as the processes of other groups that do business with you.

So how does conformance come into play with your processes? Here are a few examples:

1. A loaning service promises to respond to their customers within 24 hours after an inquiry is made.

2. A local pizza joint assures customers that they would deliver pizzas to their doorstep in 30 minutes or its free.

3. A software developer required to write a program with 10 correlated features and no more than 3 bugs per a thousand lines of written code.

4. A kitchen crew told to cook 20 steaks, 15 of which are medium rare and 5 rare.

To understand conformance better, think of archery. Let us say that every Critical to Quality metric (CTQ) is the bullseye found on every target. To conform to customer standards, you must be able to hit that bullseye with every arrow you drew.

But, of course, we can't make perfect hits every time we shoot. You may hit a perfect bullseye once and the rest will just group around the first shot.

Believe it or not, this is okay. If any product or service you offer more or less hits most of the customer's set standards, then your product is to be deemed of good quality and you are deemed a consistent provider of such. Going back to the archery scenario, you are considered a good marksman if your shots group the bullseye.

But what happens if one of your shots was way off? Perhaps it did not even hit near the bullseye. Or perhaps it was so off-angle that it did not even hit the target.

This is a deviation from the standard. The outlier. That one freak occurrence where you did not meet the customer's expectations. This is what is called as Process Deviation.

Is Minimizing Variation Enough?

So, if you have little process variation, does this mean that you are hitting all of the needs of the customers? Not really. A more consistent process simply means that everyone managed to follow the process to the letter but the process itself does not assure that value is ultimately delivered to the customer.

When quality issues happen, you have to first determine whether or not it was caused by a variation in the process or some inherent flaw in the system. Things like a lack of training, old equipment, and mere negligence can cause problems. But, fortunately, they are easy to address since they are rather obvious manifestations.

However, if the system itself is flawed, the problem instantly doubles in size. Instead of having to merely do quick fixes, you now have to consider the idea of having to redesign your entire process.

To make a good judgement call on this situation, black belts and master black belts must clearly define the process and determine whether the problem was created by any of the wasteful activities mentioned earlier in this chapter or it was caused by a deviation from the process.

And the latter can be quite challenging to determine as you have to carefully track workflows, the allocation of responsibilities, and the formulated standards to get to the source of the problem.

Of course, the conclusions you can come up with are just as good as your interpretation of the data as provided. And if your information is not accurate, the best that you can do in addressing the situation is, well, get lucky.

Can Variation be Eliminated?

The answer, sadly, is one big NO. Unless your business process is found in a work environment where outside variables have little impact, there is always some process variation occurring. Let us say, for the sake of discussion, that you promised to deliver pizzas within 30 minutes after an order is placed.

What happens if there was heavy traffic going to that client's place? What if the delivery truck blew a tire or you were pulled to the site by patrolmen because of a faulty taillight? Surely, these would affect how you deliver on your promises.

Or what if you had contingencies like a spare vehicle or you knew some shortcuts in that place? They might help in you delivering your promises within the acceptable limit, but they won't always assure 100% success in that particular situation.

Reducing Process over Results

This can be rather counter-intuitive, but it is best that you focus on consistency over getting results. Why? You ask. Isn't the whole point of being in the business to produce great results?

Going back to the archery scenario, even the hits that group around your most accurate shot are still variations of the process. Unless you have the skills of Robin Hood, it is statistically impossible to get all shots hitting the bullseye with 100% accuracy.

But what if we had two archers? Let us say that Archer A varies his strategy every shoot. He might aim from the left in one shot, he might shoot from above in the other. He might even do handstands and draw his bow with his feet. But he keeps hitting the target.

And then we have Archer B. He stands on the same spot and aims his bow in exactly the same angle. He may score a perfect hit one or two times but the rest of his shots group around an area near the bullseye.

Which of the archers has the best chance of improving their accuracy and consistency? The answer is Archer B.

The reason for this is simple: He always sticks to the same process. This makes him easy to analyze and predict. Thus, you can set up a process map that allows you to detect where he makes the most and correct the same.

Archer A, though good, is all over the place. There is no way to identify what he is doing right when he lands a hit and where he went wrong should he ever miss a target.

Thus, by reducing variations in the process, you make the Lean Six Sigma implementation phase easier on everybody's part. As a result, what was seemingly counterproductive as a measure through reducing variations regardless of how good the results are can give your business more opportunities to expand later on.

One Important Note

What you have to understand is waste is a natural byproduct of your business's operations. If you do things wastefully, then you are bound to generate a lot of waste. It is as simple as that.

As such, you have to remember that Waste may be the focus of the Lean Six Sigma method, it is not the one that it addresses directly. After all, waste is just a manifestation of what is wrong with your business.

Thus, your chosen strategy in your Lean Six Sigma projects should be to address what was generating all that waste and variation. Because if you are going to just address the waste itself, you are merely applying the proverbial band-aid to what could be a festering wound.

For example, your production cycles generate defects by 20 to 30 items. The fault could be with your machines. It could be in your staff. It could even be in the organizational culture. You'd never know until you dig deeper.

And, eventually, you'd still end up dealing with increased business costs as well as lost time and resources. To identify waste, it is important that you analyze your organization and find out which part of the process generates the most waste.

After all, everything will be a matter of standardizing things and keeping the changes sustainable.

Chapter 10 Problems and Challenges

So, is Lean Six Sigma the best problem-solving methodology out there? Not really.

Don't get the wrong idea, though. A lot of companies have implemented Lean Six Sigma successfully and enjoyed its benefits including a better bottom line, increased productivity, and a reinvigorated workforce.

Unfortunately, others have not fared so well with Lean Six Sigma which causes the rest thinking about using the methodology themselves. So, will the methodology work on your business? That depends greatly on, well, you. But it is best that you learn everything that you have to about this methodology, even its ugly side.

Why Don't Businesses Use Lean Six Sigma at all?

There are many reasons why a lot of organizations don't use Lean Six Sigma. Many of these are unfounded but many are also rather valid. And, of course, some are based on misconceptions about the method.

Either way, here are some of the reasons blurted out by people why they won't even think about using Lean Six Sigma for their projects.

1. "It's a Fad!"

A lot of organizations don't use Lean Six Sigma because everybody else is using it. For them, LSS is similar to buzzword-heavy methodologies that rose (and fell) in recent years including Total Quality Management, Business Process Re-Engineering, and the Theory of Constraints.

And right from the premise you could get the idea that this reason is based on a rather faulty understanding of Lean Six Sigma. It's not a fad technically as the methodology has been in use by various industries for over several decades now.

What's more, Lean Six Sigma is not something that was cooked up by a boardroom meeting or a marketing session. It was first established in Japanese industries which lead to the country's huge boom during the last half of the 20th century.

And, aside from that, it is spearheaded by several industry bigwigs like Henry Ford, Western Electric's Walter Shewhart, and Toyota's Shigeo Shingo. As such, the methodology would rather not have you think that is just this hot new business administration trend.

2. "I Don't Have the Time to Dedicate to the Program"

Think about it this way: if a person is too busy putting out trash fires, would they have the time to listen to you explain to them the finer points of how to throw a pail of water in a burning pit? Time is a commodity that not all companies have the luxury of. For you, there is a strong chance that you are racing against a deadline of sorts to meet an objective.

And Lean Six Sigma does demand time from you in order to learn it. You have to devote a portion of your workday learning the basics and then create strategies on how to implement. While you are doing those, you still have to make sure that the business functions normally on a regular basis.

This is why it was recommended that the Lean Six Sigma initiative starts small and in a self-sustained unit within the organization. A few would have to master the method first so that they, in turn, can teach the rest. If done right, the entire organization can embrace the methodology without wasting too much of their time learning it.

But what if your organization could not afford to apply the LSS drive in a small scale since, well, it is already operating in a small scale? This makes for a perfect segue into the next reason which is....

3. "We're too Small!"

One oft-repeated phrase in implementing Lean Six Sigma is "we've hit a wall". That "wall" can come in many forms.

For many small businesses, that wall comes in the form of possessing cash flow that is tied up in inventory (or receivables), even when the company is generating profits. For some, that wall takes the form of persistent employee turnover. And for some, the wall could be the frustration of having to deliver a different quality of product or service than the one you and your team were used to.

Either way, the wall signifies that processes being implemented are becoming insufficient in achieving the goals that you have set.

But the thing with Lean Six Sigma is that it is highly adaptable as a methodology. In fact, it can be an Agile methodology in the sense that it allows you to perfectly embrace change, whatever form that it comes in, and still provide value to your customers.

The truth is that Lean Six Sigma never asks you to completely overhaul your current business layout. It only requires for you to completely understand how your business is performing given its current tools and systems and how that might be improved through the LSS implementation process.

And if you do think that an overhaul is needed, the LSS method is compatible enough with other methodologies that its goals can fit with what you have already set to achieve with other projects. As such, the size of your business and team composition should never become a hindrance to your projects provided, of course, that you fully understand how the Lean Six Sigma methodology must be applied.

4. "I'm Not a Manufacturer!"

Here's another Lean Six Sigma myth that still prevails today. Since it was first formed and implemented to be use in a car manufacturing facility, then Lean Six Sigma is meant only for those companies that produce something tangible that is going to be used for mechanical and industrial purposes, right? Wrong.

You'd be surprised as to how many non-manufacturing companies were able to succeed in implementing Lean Six Sigma. These include:

- ☐ The Bank of America
- ☐ Coca-Cola
- ☐ Starbucks
- ☐ Wal-Mart

☐ AT&T

The reason for this is Lean Six Sigma is actually focused on waste and process variation, something that is shared by a lot of industries. In fact, food service sectors can benefit from Lean Six Sigma more due to the more perishable nature of their products and the fact that they can generate more business waste on a relative perspective than manufacturers.

The point is that the Lean Six Sigma method should be applicable to your business if it has a fairly repeatable process or cyclical activity, where data can be collected from such activities, and there is a need to produce the same item consistently regardless if the amount of repetitions is 10 or 1 million times.

5. "I'm Not an Engineer. I Don't Do Math"

Granted, the Six Sigma part of the methodology can be rather intimidating. Statistics, after all, is a subject that many who went to college are not exactly excited about, even those that ace on it. There's just something about number crunching that is a bit of a hassle for anyone who wants their analysis to be simple and straightforward.

But here's the thing, though: you don't need to have a strong grasp of mathematics in order to enjoy the benefits of the methodology. In fact, some of the most effective tools of the Lean Six Sigma arsenal like drawing a process map or a fishbone diagram requires your team to have a good pair of eyes (and a lot of common sense) in order to be properly utilized.

The diagrams are easy enough to put up and using them to identify bottlenecks and other problem areas are equally easy. Even asking the simple question of "why?" can yield you a lot of possible answers. The point is that you must never forget to understand what the consumer really needs in order to reduce waste and variance in the business process.

6. "We're Using Lean Already. Thank You"

Some businesses do not use Lean Six Sigma since they are using Lean already. Some even state that they are using Lean Six Sigma but would focus more on the Lean aspect.

However, Lean and Six Sigma are not exclusive concepts, nor do they need to be applied in a linear way. They, by design, can complement one another.

Lean speeds up the entire process while Six Sigma makes it more accurate. Lean reduces the waste produced by the inherent flaws in your system while Six Sigma reduces the probabilities of that one freak defect from happening in every successive good production run.

To put it on simpler terms, Lean is all about Efficiency while Six Sigma is all about Effectiveness. And those two things tend to produce dramatic results if you focus on them both. If you focus on Lean, you sacrifice quality for speed. Likewise, you sacrifice efficiency if you focus on Six Sigma.

7. "We Tried, and It Didn't Work out for Us"

Any business owner or project manager that uses this reason should ask themselves "Why did I fail?". Perhaps the fault lies in the people and the technology. Or perhaps it was the intentions behind the implementation of the initiative.

And what about the commitment levels of everyone involved in it? How did you define success and what were its metrics? Were the goals even realistic in the first place?

The point is that this is more of a problem of execution rather than an inherent flaw in the method. And if you do fail in applying the Lean Six Sigma methodology, there is always the option to get back to the drawing board. Just remember that any tool is just as effective as the people who use it.

The concept is rather simple and straightforward that you should get considerable results from it if only you and your team tried to understand the basics.

8. "I'm Afraid of Change and Failure"

This is perhaps the most legitimate and understandable. The only problem is that a lot of people would not admit of such and thus bluster their way out of even giving the method a chance.

Pride is indeed a factor, however, when you think about it dread and fear are more potent emotions. It may be paralyzing to the point that you can't implement any change that you want to see in the business out of fear that you are going to mess things up.

It prevents your team from learning new skills, taking on new roles, or implement more agile programs like the Lean Six Sigma methodology. If you want to succeed in Lean Six Sigma, or any other Agile methodology, that Fear must be eliminated.

Common Implementation Mistakes

Another aspect you should consider in the Lean Six Sigma method is its actual application in your project. What is barely mentioned by a lot of people is that there are a number of pitfalls that stand in your way of properly implementing the process.

And as we have mentioned a while ago in this chapter, no discussion of Lean Six Sigma is ever complete without addressing some of the mistakes that you could potentially make in implementing your strategies and how you could overcome such. And here are some of them:

1. Thinking Certifications are Enough

In order to make everyone in your Lean Six Sigma team as competent as possible, you might hire people who are trained and certified under the Lean Six Sigma methodology. And you think to yourself that these certified people are most definitely able contribute to the implementation phase.

But keep in mind that there is more to Lean Six Sigma than just certifications. If your team is more focused on becoming certified, you run the risk of doing things too by-the-book. This means that your team gets more tied up to doing things through set procedures rather than asking how the system could be improved for the better.

This could also come back to bite you in the rear later on when your initial trainees become mentors themselves. If they are too focused on the certification, they can't provide really valuable tactical advice to new yellow and green belts assigned to new Lean Six Sigma projects.

The Solution

If possible, train your Lean Six Sigma team to focus more on understanding customer specifications than doing things by the sequence. They should understand that the LSS method should adapt to the specifications of the project or the goals of the group, not the other way around.

And this is where your skills as the primary mentor would come into importance. You must know how and when to apply the tools provided and even provide constructive criticism if you feel that the team is becoming too focused on becoming certified, not adaptable.

2. Indifferent Higher Ups

You would think that resistance would come the most from people directly underneath you in the organizational chart but no. When it comes to convincing people that Lean Six Sigma works, employees are more than willing to give it the chance.

It is a senior manager who is so convinced that it won't be applicable to organization (and for the various reasons stated above, to boot) that would be your major source of frustration in the implementation process.

The reason for this is simple; the higher ups have a lot of influence in dictating how many people should become LSS certified and the overall scope of the initiative. In other words, their support can make or break the initiative irrespective of available resources.

The Solution

At this instance, your best strategy is to be diplomatic. After all, you still report to these people and you'd rather not derail the effort further by antagonizing them.

You have to be forthcoming with what the method requires and the benefits the company can enjoy from it. Its role should be emphasized and any misconception regarding the method should be sufficiently addressed.

If possible, have a meeting set up with the higher ups so you could explain the Lean Six Sigma methodology to them in a direct and open communication channel. There's no assurance that you can convince theme here, mind you. But at least you can explain the concept to terms easier to understand which sets up a future acceptance.

3. A Faulty Strategy

Regardless of the nature of your operations, it is still important that you synchronize your business goals to the goals of the Lean Six Sigma initiative. As such, a faulty strategy and misaligned goals will result in confusion among teams and the higher ups which prevents the organization from delivering the value they promised to customers.

If not addressed, this could reduce the overall effectiveness of all teams. Delays would start appearing, customers get frustrated, and everyone in the organization would start to question what was the point of Lean Six Sigma in the first place.

The Solution

As the project manager, you must make it a point to constantly align the goals of the Lean Six Sigma project with its core principles. This means that you must scrutinize the strategies to be implemented before the date of actual execution. Talk with your team constantly before the implementation phase starts. What are their concerns? Is there a problem that they have yet to air out? Maintain the line of communication between your teams as open as possible so that everybody understands the overall strategy to be implemented.

One key aspect to remember here is that the strategy should be tied to the changes in business results. This means that you have to monitor the implementation properly and the overall goals should be constantly remembered by all teams involved.

4. Selecting the Wrong Lean Six Sigma Project

A lack of project prioritization makes the team run the risk of wasting valuable resources. Aside from that, this results in processes becoming prioritized at a period earlier than expected as well as bottlenecks. Worse, your green and yellow belts might have to deal with tasks that they were not yet trained for resulting in haphazard results.

Whatever the case, not properly selecting which LSS project to complete first or simultaneously with the others can lead to lost time, money, and other valuable resources. This would even lead to a delivery of poor quality or delays in the completion of projects.

The Solution

During the training phase, it is important to take as much time as possible in helping the trainees understand how to prioritize tasks. You should hammer in the point that, yes, all projects are important, but they must be done in the right sequence, so you don't create unnecessary waste.

It would even be recommended that you take a leaf out of the Kanban process here and come up with a project scheduling scheme. Divide all projects into 3 groups: Proposed, Doing, and Done. This table will shift every time a new project is proposed or is completed.

With this Kanban visual signaling system, you and your team can have an understand of what needs to be done now and how that correlates to projects in the future.

5. Lack of Support and Collaboration

Where a lot of Lean Six Sigma teams fail is in making sure that everybody in the organization is in on the effort of implementing the method. This could be attributed to the team failing to properly communicate the benefits of Lean Six Sigma or it could be due to the failure of laying down the formal rules and guidelines in which the end goals are to be attained. Either way, everybody is just doing their own thing in the organization which leads to wasted efforts or, worse, huge losses.

The Solution

There is no other workaround for this problem but to make sure that the Lean Six Sigma initiative slowly works itself to becoming a part of the organizational culture. To be more blunt about it, you have to lay down the concept that what the organization truly wants and what Lean Six Sigma can offer are basically one and the same.

For instance, the organization wants to increase profit margins while optimizing the systems to becoming efficient. Lean Six Sigma is a method that can achieve those by removing waste and variance while also simplifying the process. If you can make the higher-ups and the stakeholders see that the conflict between organizational needs and Lean Six Sigma goals is just a matter of semantics, they are more inclined to support it.

Important Note: The rule of thumb when addressing implementation issues is always "The earlier, the better". You have to know when the organization is about to create a mistake in its Lean Six Sigma initiative and find ways to address it. If you take to long to address an issue, you run the risk of bloating the problem until it becomes too expensive to fix.

Mastering Lean Six Sigma

As was stated, the Lean Six Sigma method is just as good as the people implementing it. So, how is your group going to master it for your various projects?

Psychologist came up with 4 stages on how a person develops competency or learns a new skill. This is based on two dimensions which is a person's level of consciousness and their current competence.

Stage 1: Unconsciously Incompetent - At this point, a person does not understand how to do something or is unable to recognize that a problem exists. In short, you don't know what you don't know. In the Lean Six Sigma perspective, this means that you are not even aware of what Lean Six Sigma is and most definitely don't know how to apply it for your project.

Stage 2: Unconsciously Incompetent - This is the point you reach when you are aware that you do not know something or how to address a problem. This is the instance when the Lean Six Sigma method is introduced to you and you realize that there is a better way of addressing a situation. In essence, you have an idea of the solution but have yet to know how to implement it in your organization.

Stage 3: Consciously Incompetent - Here, whoever was teaching the group has demonstrate the skill and knowledge needed to implement to methodology, but it requires a lot of concentration and effort. This is a stage that usually happens when going through the Green and Yellow belt training.

In essence, the trainees now understand the methodology and how to use the tools, but it will take a lot of practice and discipline in order to become a master of the methodology. This is a rather critical stage of the learning process as you'd want to internalize the process. Without mastering the basics, you and your team run the risk of reverting to your previous standards and failed methodologies.

Stage 4: Unconsciously Competent - After putting in much time and effort in mastering the method, Lean Six Sigma has become second nature to the person. They can now implement it with minimal mistakes and can adjust their strategies to respond to sudden changes in customer specifications.

But, again, it takes a while to get to this stage. You need to master the method by applying it several times in different projects. Sure, you are going to make a lot of mistakes, but you can use those as opportunities to hone your craft. You can also undergo further training, read more Lean Six Sigma books, and attend meetings.

If you yourself feel confident enough to teach others how to master the skill or even do some presentations yourself, then you will know that you have finally reached this stage.

How Do I Continuously Improve?

You have to understand that Lean Six Sigma is not a one-off thing that you could forget about in time. It is the most effective not only if you have mastered it but also continuously seek ways to develop yourself.

Continuous Improvement is one of the major goals of any Lean Six Sigma initiative apart from eliminating waste and process variances. The question is, how should you do it? For starters, Continuous Improvement should not be seen as a strategy. Instead, it should be a way of life. A discipline, if you may.

And to maintain this way of life, there are a few tips that you should keep in mind.

1. Focus on Small Steps

This might sound counterproductive, but it is better if you can put more focus on the smaller, incremental changes that your business or group makes over the massive shifts done over a long period of time. The reason for this is simple: small changes are done quickly, regularly, and are rather inexpensive. By completing a set of daily tasks, you can see the changes take place as they occur.

More importantly, a focus on small changes removes the psychological barrier that prevents you from continuously improving. Think about it: When it comes to implementing changes, the first complaint that you or your team would utter would go along the lines "why is it taking so long for the benefits to come?" It can be frustrating at times to think that your efforts are seemingly not paying off which could kill the Lean Six Sigma initiative at its earliest phases.

But, with small changes, you and your team could see and reap the benefits and celebrate each victory earlier on. In time, you'll see the changes accumulate until you would notice your organization is in a far better state than what you started with.

2. Empower Employees

Yes, you and other leaders have a lot of influence in making Lean Six Sigma work but it's the employees that would make it successful. One key problem as to why Lean Six Sigma initiatives fail is that nobody down the line knows the principles by heart. As a result, they won't realize that the way they do things currently are not optimized or that there are more efficient ways to do their tasks.

Alternatively, a lot of people are resistant to change because change brings about uncertainty. Lastly, some are just reluctant to share ideas out of fear that they are going to be placed in the limelight.

It is your role, then, to educate your people on the tools and techniques as well as choosing the best ones for certain situations. But most importantly, you have to give them the assurance that there is nothing to fear out of trying something new.

The less reluctant your team is towards embracing the method, the quicker they can master it and move through the Lean Six Sigma ranks.

3. Feedback Always Matters

It goes without saying that everybody within the team should be encouraged to voice out their concerns as the Lean Six Sigma initiative is being implemented. You have to have a little bit of dissent within your teams not because you want people to undermine the rest of the group's efforts.

Instead, you need some people to remind everybody else that maybe, just maybe, all of you are going about this problem the wrong way. Seeing things from multiple perspectives allow you to detect problems before they get worse and course correct. But such feedback would not be available if people just keep to themselves.

Maintain an open and transparent line of communication between teams and management during the initiative and you should get the best possible results from the program.

To Summarize

Now, would these problems occur at your implementation phase? Or do the reasons above apply to your situation? Not exactly. There is no doubt that some Lean Six Sigma initiatives went smoothly and others, well, didn't.

That being said, it is still important to know that there will be flaws in your execution. After all, if you don't think that you are going to fail, you can't properly prepare a contingency in case that you do. And if you do fail, then at the very least you and your team could use that instance as an opportunity to learn and do better next time.

Conclusion

I'd like to thank you for transiting my lines from start to finish.

I hope this book was able to help you to understand the principles of Lean Six Sigma.

As of this point, there should be no doubt that the Lean Six Sigma methodology is effective. Sure, it might have some few flaws but that does not take away from its overall potential to optimize your organization's current process methodology.

But you might be wondering whether or not Lean Six Sigma is right for your organization. In other words, you might have no doubts that Lean Six Sigma works but would it work for your business or organization specifically?

If you still have any doubts whether or not Lean Six Sigma is the best option for your upcoming projects, it is best that you answer a few questions first.

What is the Goal of the Group/Business?

Regardless of what industry it operates in or the kind of products it offers, any organization has one goal to achieve:

enjoy more from doing less. This does not mean that they cut corners or cheap out on their output, mind you.

The goal of every organization out there is to bring value to the customer without overextending themselves. And this is where Waste becomes an important factor as it the biggest manifestation that some areas of the process are not optimized.

Aside from showing the flaws of the system, waste does ultimately affect the quality of the end product. If only those wasteful activities and variations in the process were eliminated, you could have come up with a better offering to the market.

And this is something that Lean Six Sigma is quite good at. If helps you identify what goes wrong and where in the process and then come up with strategies that directly address such. In time and with support, that problem could either be minimized or eliminated.

What are Your Personal Goals?

On a personal level, you should also consider what you want to do in your chosen profession or career. For many, career growth could be either in movement or security. To put it in other words, there are those that want to stay in a rather lucrative position for as long as possible or move through a series of highly rewarding jobs and positions over various sectors in a considerably quick pace.

This is where a Lean Six Sigma certification would come in important as the methodology is widely recognized by various industries and sectors in the market. And, as far as upper management is concerned, they would like to invest on someone who knows how to optimize systems and deliver on the specifications of a project.

And if you are already in a position of considerable influence or power, the Lean Six Sigma certification could still help you make yourself relevant in the organization's strategic decision-making sessions. When it comes to eliminating waste or delivering value, your input would have a considerable weight in them which means that they are more likely to be implemented. And if that implementation was successful, the success could be attributed to you.

In other words, with the credentials offered by a Lean Six Sigma program, you can secure your tenure in any organization or allow yourself to move quickly through the ranks and reap more benefits.

But, of course, this is only possible if you continuously learn and improve. A Yellow belt in Lean Six Sigma is already good but the Green, Black, and Master Black belts will put you in more favorable positions.

Aside from that, credentials might be good, but they won't do you any favors if they don't allow you to be successful. What good is a Black Belt certification, for instance, if every project you have led has either generated mediocre results or was dropped because of delays and technical problems?

As such, the ultimate indicator of your mastery of the Lean Six Sigma method is not exactly your rank but your ability to apply what you have learned in actual scenarios. And that whatever you applied was actually effective and sustainable.

Are You Open to the Prospect of Change?

Change is a but a part of the natural order. However, a lot of managers tend to balk at it because of the uncertainty it brings. Why change something that has been proven to work?

But you have to remember that there is always a better way to do things and that there are issues that have to be fixed to enhance a system. This is what the Lean Six Sigma methodology is rather good it.

Through analysis, it brings problems that you were not aware of or, at least, deemed to be insignificant and then lay out the ways on how they could affect the process. By understanding how one thing leads to another, a Lean Six Sigma professional can map out a better flow of processes so that value is delivered to the customer at a more efficient rate.

As such, if you are not a believer of “If it isn’t broke, don’t fix it” and are always seeking for ways to develop yourself or your organization, then Lean Six Sigma might be a good fit for you.

And now we come to the end of this book. Now that you have understood the basics of the Lean Six Sigma methodology, all that is left to do is to get the proper training, get certified, and start applying all that you have learned.

If done right, you might just improve yourself and your organizational processes in such a way that you can deliver on the output that you have promised to clients; and on time to boot.

I wish you the best of luck!

Thank you

Before you go, I just wanted to say thank you for purchasing my book.

You could have picked from dozens of other books on the same topic but you took a chance and chose this one.

So, a HUGE thanks to you for getting this book and for reading all the way to the end.

Now I wanted to ask you for a small favor. ***Could you please consider posting a review on the platform? Reviews are one of the easiest ways to support the work of independent authors.***

This feedback will help me continue to write the type of books that will help you get the results you want. So if you enjoyed it, please let me know!

Resources

Books

M. Adams (2004). Lean Six Sigma: A Tools Guide. Air Academy Associates

T. Stern (2018). Lean Six Sigma: International Standards and Global Guidelines. Productivity Press

N. Decarlo (2007). The Complete Idiot's Guide to Lean Six Sigma. Alpha Books

D. Pomfret (2009). Lean Project Management: A Study of Application. Project Management Institute

T. MacAdam (2009). Lean Project Management: Slashing Waste to Reduce Project Costs and Timelines. Project Management Institute

M. Thomsett (2005). Getting Started in Six Sigma. Wiley

L. Tang (2003). Six Sigma: Advanced Tools for Black Belts and Master Black Belts. Wiley

J. Arthur (2007). Lean Six Sigma Demystified. Mcgraw-Hill

R. Pirasteh-R. Fox (2011). Profitability with no Boundaries: Optimizing TOC, Lean, Six Sigma Results: Focus, Reduce Waste, Contain Variability. ASQ Quality Press

M. George (2002). Lean Six Sigma: Combining Six Sigma Quality with Lean Speed. McGraw-Hill Europe,

Videos

TECOEnergyinc. (2016. June 10). Lean: 8 Wastes. Retrieved From: **https://www.youtube.com/watch?v=VWN8NrJ7LE8**

fkiQuality. (2018. April 1). 5 Steps DMAIC Overview: Green Belt 2.0 Lean Six Sigma. Retrieved from: **https://www.youtube.com/watch?v=go7KMaKV-W8**

Gemba Academy. (2009. March 10). Learn What 5S is and How it Applies to Any Industry. Retrieved from: **https://www.youtube.com/watch?v=c0Q-xaYior0**

Lean Lab. (2017. April 24). What is Continuous Improvement? 4 Points to Create the CI Culture. Retrieved from:

https://www.youtube.com/watch?v=sWj9MowzDV0

Websites

Six Sigma Daily. (2014. June 12). Six Sigma Belt Levels and Related Training. Retrieved from: **https://www.sixsigmadaily.com/six-sigma-training-belt-levels/**

Kainexus Blog (2018. September 27). 13 Indispensable Lean Six Sigma Tools and Techniques. Retrieved From: **https://blog.kainexus.com/improvement-disciplines/six-sigma/six-sigma-tools/13-indispensable-six-sigma-tools-and-techniques**

Lifehack.Org (2019. May 28). How to Declutter Your Life and Reduce Stress (The Ultimate Guide). Retrieved from: **https://www.lifehack.org/articles/lifestyle/how-to-declutter-your-life-and-reduce-stress.html**

www.ingramcontent.com/pod-product-compliance
Lightning Source LLC
Chambersburg PA
CBHW071416210326
41597CB00020B/3536